Responses and Insights to the Value of This Book

"A concise summary of the relationships that constitute the arts ecosystem, presented in such a way that will be valuable for partnership development and arts advocacy. I particularly appreciate the references to rural communities and expect this book will remain close at hand as I work on strategies and tools, both from an economic development perspective as well as with a focus on secondary cultural development, for arts advocacy in rural and remote communities."

Felicity Buckell

Conseil des arts Temiskaming Arts Council, Ontario (Canada)

"I am impressed at how Ms. Proctor has gathered the pertinent arguments on the broad benefits of supporting the arts, along with some good practical suggestions on how to do so."

Diane Davy

Executive Director, Work in Culture, Ontario (Canada)

"As a smart, easy reference guide for arts and cultural managers, this book is brimming with tested, practical strategies anyone can use to create sturdy partnerships, allies and purposeful relationships in their communities."

Nathan Medd

Managing Director, Banff Centre for Arts and Creativity, Alberta (Canada)

"Ms. Proctor's handbook is an excellent partnership development tool that will help artists and arts administrators communicate the value of cultural products and experiences as being 'worth paying for'. By expanding support for artists, we will no doubt positively impact community development as well as our collective health and well-being."

"Bravo for facilitating this very important conversation that may have developmental applications in other sectors!"

Donald Arsenault (Retired)

Social Development Officer and Manager, Government of Canada

"The author (Cate) brings to light challenges and practical solutions facing arts administrators, artists and indeed the broader entertainment and sports sector. The reader benefits from these perspectives as well as realizing that we within the sector are not alone in facing these challenges. We are a community."

Tom Moser

Partner - Global Marketing Partners, Florida (USA)

"Few arts administrators arrive on the job with MBA training. Most of us get here via a tangential path: often through community development or our own artistic practice. We veer into arts administration without a lot of preparation because we love the arts, but do not anticipate that the work can be thankless, and the demands relentless. Cate Proctor's guide for administrators will help ease the burden. It clearly lays out key factors that determine success: understanding the cultural ecosystem and its diverse stakeholders, appreciating the value of our own organization, assessing the value of our assets and how to maximize support. The book reminds us of things we know, at least intuitively, offers practical new tools, and guides the reader through a process of strategic evaluation."

"Many of the case studies involve small operations and rural communities. It is a rule of thumb that smaller arts organizations, particularly when located far from an urban centre, are likely to be run by a small team – perhaps a single person – valiantly juggling administration, promotion, social media, grant writing and managing core activities. The work is by turns exhilarating and exhausting. Cate Proctor's guide provides practical insights, useful statistical, implementable strategies, and a reassuring voice to help the beleaguered administrator. All of this in a format that is accessible in its style and streamlined size."

Guy Rogers
Executive Director, English Language Arts Network, Quebec (Canada)

Leverage the Arts Ecosystem to Influence Local Prosperity

A Partnership Guide for Arts Administrators
and Community Builders

M. Catherine Proctor MBA

1st Edition

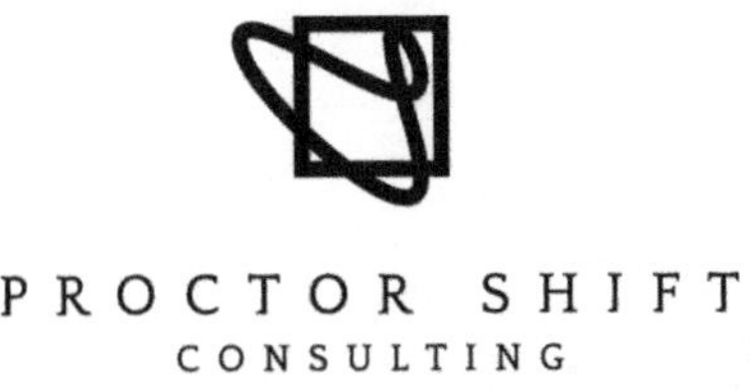

PROCTOR SHIFT
CONSULTING

Ottawa, Ontario (Canada)

Leverage the Arts Ecosystem to Influence Local Prosperity:
A Partnership Guide for Arts Administrators and Community
Builders.

Published by
Proctor Shift Consulting
www.proctorshiftconsulting.com

A copy of this book is retained by Library and Archives
Canada.

Copyright ©Proctor Shift Consulting, 2020.

All Rights Reserved. No part of this work, including the
exterior and interior design and icons, may be reproduced,
stored in a retrieval system or transmitted in any form, by
any means (electronic, photocopying, mechanical recording,
or otherwise) without the prior written permission of the
copyright holder, except to include brief quotations in a
review.

ISBN Print Edition: 978-1-9992766-0-7
ISBN PDF Ebook Edition: 978-1-9992766-1-4

Proctor Shift Consulting
Founder | Principal: M. Catherine Proctor, MBA
Email: cate@proctorshiftconsulting.com
Website: www.proctorshiftconsulting.com

TABLE OF CONTENTS

FOREWORD — 1

DEDICATION — 5

ABOUT THE AUTHOR — 7

ACKNOWLEDGEMENTS — 11

DISCLAIMER — 13

INTRODUCTION — 15

THE ARTS ECOSYSTEM — 17
HOW TO READ THIS BOOK — 20

BACKGROUND — 23

THE FOCUS MATRIX — 23

PART 1. WHAT YOU NEED TO KNOW ABOUT THE ARTS ECOSYSTEM — 29

1. PEELING BACK: CREATIVE INDUSTRIES AND ECONOMIC GROWTH — 29

CASE STUDY: RIVER ARTS DISTRICT, ASHEVILLE, NORTH CAROLINA, USA — 43

2. ARTS ADMINISTRATORS: HUB OF THE ARTS ECOSYSTEM — 47

3. THE ARTS ECOSYSTEM: UNDERSTANDING SEGMENTATION — 57

CASE STUDY: KIM'S CONVENIENCE — 73

4. BRIDGING THE GAP: ARTISTS-TO-CREATIVE INDUSTRIES — 77

GAINING CROSS-SECTORAL SUPPORT — 78
ARTISTS PLAY THE LONG GAME — 83
CASE STUDY: ANNE OF GREEN GABLES BY LUCY MAUD MONTGOMERY — 98

5. ARTISTS: PRIMARY DRIVERS OF THE ARTS ECOSYSTEM — 101

SIX ARTISTIC DRIVERS — 102
SEVEN STAKEHOLDERS — 103
KEY RESEARCH FINDINGS: DEVELOPING A VIBRANT ARTS ECOSYSTEM — 105

6. BENEFITS THAT ARTISTS INFLUENCE — 113

THE ARTIST AS THE CRITICAL DRIVER/PRINCIPAL STAKEHOLDER — 115
ARTS ORGANIZATIONS AND ARTS SECTOR INTERMEDIARIES — 117
HERITAGE AND MUSEUMS — 119

RESIDENTS   120

MUNICIPALITY   122

BUSINESS   124

PROVINCIAL/STATE GOVERNMENT   126

CASE STUDY: "OPEN HOUSE" IN YORK, ALABAMA. ARTIST: MATTHEW MAZZOTTA   130

PART 2. APPLYING RESEARCH AND DEVELOPING STRATEGIES   **133**

7. INTERSECTING DRIVERS AND STAKEHOLDERS   **133**

ARTISTIC DRIVER #1: CREATIVE WORKS   136

ARTISTIC DRIVER #2: PLACE   149

CASE STUDY: ART IN THE OPEN, ESTABLISHING A CONTEMPORARY ARTS FESTIVAL   161

ARTISTIC DRIVER #3: LINKAGES TO THE ARTS ECOSYSTEM   163

ARTISTIC DRIVER #4: NON-FINANCIAL RESOURCES   181

ARTISTIC DRIVER #5: VISIONING   190

ARTISTIC DRIVER #6: ECONOMICS   201

ARTISTIC DRIVER #7: EDUCATION (POST-SECONDARY)   211

CASE STUDY: QUIDI VIDI PLANTATION, NEWFOUNDLAND, CANADA   217

8. YOUR UNIQUE ASSETS   **221**

DEVELOPING AND ORGANIZING YOUR PRIORITIES   226

BUILDING PARTNERSHIPS THAT SUPPORT STRATEGIC TARGETS AND OBJECTIVES   230

CASE STUDY: COMMUNITY GARDEN, OTTAWA LITTLE THEATRE, ONTARIO, CANADA   243

9. LET'S GET SOCIAL!   **247**

THE ARTS IMPACT EVERYONE, BUILDING VALUE—DAILY!   253

10. IN CONCLUSION: THE (UNTHINKABLE) ALTERNATIVE   **259**

AFTERWORD   **263**

REFERENCES (BY CHAPTER)   **267**

GENERAL REFERENCES   **276**

END NOTES   **280**

Foreword

This book presents a unique perspective on the value that the arts brings to society and the dynamic flow of artistic creations through the arts ecosystem. As an arts administrator, an arts sector consultant, and an entrepreneur, its author, Cate Proctor, is among the select few who can bridge the space between the artistic mind and its intrinsic value. She sees clearly how the creative origin of an idea is connected to the large-scale benefits that can accrue to the community and society.

I had a dream to run a production company, but I held zero knowledge of the industry that intrigued me, and no industry existed to support film and television in my community. As time passed, I began to understand that everything I did required creative puzzle making. I orchestrated artists, co-producers, networks, and governments to work together to see both their individual and mutual gain. I sought others to learn storytelling, which was and is key to generating others' interest. I knowingly developed partnerships, established trust, and attracted buy-in from co-producers with more experience than me, realizing broadcasters would license these stories. I learned over time.

My company, Cellar Door Productions Inc., produced an animation of *The True Meaning of Crumbfest* and developed a pilot with Chef Michael Smith that eventually became *The Inn Chef*, a TV series that ran from 1998 to 2000 which then spawned other shows in this series. Each project required writers, voice actors, and musicians for original scores. We also needed creative design, post-production for sound and editing, and full-service animation companies. We serviced two new television networks: TeleTOON and The Food Network. My company grew, developed other properties and partnerships, and distributed to networks around the world.

There is business in art, and it is big business! Many profit from it and many benefit from it. For example, a ripple effect developed in my local community from my business. The city's downtown core benefitted. Businesses and rentals suppliers that serviced rural productions emerged. More chef-inspired restaurants opened.

I realized I was developing intellectual property (IP), and that IP is everything. Why? Because it is the golden asset. When Cellar Door Productions Inc. began, new financial incentives from a then burgeoning provincial government allowed me to maintain ownership of my company's creative IP. Although artistic IP belongs to its creator, leveraging creative capital (e.g., a person's IP) through further adaptations is money in the bank.

Creative capital is a creative idea. Through creative expression, idea development and expanded presentation, economic and social impacts evolve into cultural capital. Like any preliminary resource, creative capital needs nurturing and investment at the early stage of development.

Creative thinking can lead to amazing things, but only if you do something with it. The creative idea you never implement will neither help you nor anyone else. It can't. Creative thinking needs to be exposed—be given wings—to affect anything.

Steve Jobs famously said, "Real artists ship." He was referring to everyone having ideas, but real artists deliver on them or 'ship.'

Culture is active. It grows with our collaborations, innovations, and enterprise, whether it be the genius of an artist viewing the world from a unique perspective or the way a community works together to host a local festival.

Cate's partnership guide is an exceptional resource. I would like to have had this reference when I was actively producing. It lays out in an easy-to-read format the importance of learning how to work together. In doing so, we can foster and sustain culture and its diversity. Cate shows clearly how citizens, arts organizations, businesses, interest groups, and government all have important roles to play.

Creativity is the heart of cultural growth. It is both the spark and the ability to ignite that spark. We do it together. In partnership.

A rising tide lifts all boats.

Gretha Rose, President
Cellar Door Production Inc.

Dedication

This book is dedicated to arts administrators. You develop, manage, and envision platforms for core artistic creators to present their artwork. You are change-makers in the lives of artists, volunteers, patrons, subscribers, workshop attendees, your communities, your staff, and your Boards of Directors. Your role is not for the faint of heart and your incredible dedication to your work does not go unnoticed.

THANK YOU!

About the Author

Catherine (Cate) Proctor, MBA

I grew up in the community of Mermaid in the small, Canadian maritime province of Prince Edward Island (PEI). Yes, this is a real place in a rural community complete with *Welcome* signs presenting the image of a mermaid. Perhaps growing up in such a place was a harbinger (in the mystical sense) that anything is possible!

From an early age, my musical talents were groomed. I took a short foray into community acting during my 20s, but my career developed into a supporting role for artists. I recognized my own pragmatism, curiosity, and strategic sensibilities and took advantage of these skills to forge new paths and measures. I developed a holistic, long-term view of the arts ecosystem and how it is intrinsically connected to people, business, and sustainability frameworks. I saw the value of helping arts organizations and artists thrive and sought to leverage my creativity, knowledge, and business principles to benefit many stakeholders, primarily artists.

My arts sector management career officially launched when I was hired as executive director of a struggling arts centre hub in PEI. The organization was on the verge of bankruptcy. Eighteen months later, operations were back in the black. Whew! It was a *lot* of work. I was so tired but *SO* invigorated. Through this experience, I saw unlimited potential within the arts ecosystem. I knew I wanted to do more--perhaps push the limits of possibility even further.

I saw how artists, local businesses, residents, the media, and others could strategically weave each other's expertise into new, expanded opportunities for success. I also knew a significant challenge was a lack of capacity (time and resources) within arts organizations. I realized that opportunities relied on relationships of trust and cooperation as much as on end results. I was convinced these relationships would support operations and increase curiosity, improve financial outcomes, and generate the potential for partnerships. I intuitively knew that applying new revenues toward increased capacity (i.e., staff) would contribute to the expansion of artists' creative outputs.

That was the plan...and it worked! The results were not a solo achievement, however. I am grateful to staff, colleagues, and board members for trusting me while I tested my theories and we learned from each other. Together, we achieved new heights.

I entered the University of Prince Edward Island Executive Master of Business Administration (EMBA) program without an undergraduate degree; I still don't have one. I was introduced to peer-reviewed articles (meaning rigorously evaluated research). Academic knowledge reflecting arts sector stakeholders, economics, and sector tensions caught my attention. My toolbox continued to fill.

With the combination of hands-on experience in arts administration, creative industry roles (television production), and formal research, I felt confident to establish a consulting management practice. I've since influenced creative cultural sector development and established my own principles to influence arts organizations' publicity, budgets, revenues, partnerships, programming, and fundraising results. In my consulting practice, I've guided non-profit arts and cultural organizations to weather challenges, close gaps, and develop opportunities. Through participation in various initiatives directed by arts sector service organizations, my consulting practice, and as a member of Arts Consultants Canada, I continue to support the value of artistic expression. I advocate for artist's creative skills, insights, and output as well as subsequent creative, societal, and economic impacts.

Surveys and other studies continue to highlight a need for business skills, partnerships, and communications within arts administration roles. I feel now is the time to share what I have learned. I hope the insights I've gained prove valuable to my readers.

And the mystique of the mermaid continues to burn bright within!

M. Catherine (Cate) Proctor

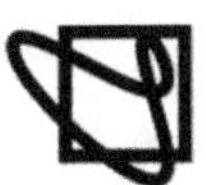

PROCTOR SHIFT
CONSULTING
LinkedIn:
https://www.linkedin.com/in/cateproctor/
Proctor Shift Consulting:
https://www.proctorshiftconsulting.com

Acknowledgements

I am appreciative for the insights I gathered from a broad spectrum of arts ecosystem professionals who acted as advance reviewers for this book. Their expertise spans the arts sector, community development, government, arts administration, and business. Their reviews, advice, and willingness to add one more request to their never-ceasing to-do list is deeply appreciated. Thank you all!

Professor Tim Carroll at the University of Prince Edward Island pushed my critical thinking skills to new levels as I pursued extensive research in fulfillment of my Executive Master of Business Administration (EMBA) degree. *The Focus Matrix* tool that emerged from academic research gathered for my EMBA Signature Paper enabled the analysis that appears in this book.

Additional research was incorporated into this book from consulting projects, websites, reports, scholarly papers, articles, and interviews. I have not attempted to cite all sources and authorities that contributed; a list of key references is provided in the References and General References sections.

My knowledge and leadership capacities in arts administration are informed through active participation on Boards of Directors, in projects and festivals, and in related career activities. Thank you to all who positively influenced this publication one way or another.

Virginia McGowan PhD (McGowan & Co.: The Write Edit Group) encouraged me to share my knowledge through a book. She acted as my copyeditor, mentor, and enthusiastic champion.

Her own publication *Harness the Power of Mentoring* had a significant influence on my approach to this publication. Thank you for everything, Ginny! You exemplify what being a mentor means!

Elena Herweyer designed my book cover. Her career pivoted from a professionally-trained visual artist to owner of an award-winning design company: Art Fresh Inc. She eloquently captured the essence of this book, conveying the layering and navigating of relationships within the arts ecosystem. I am grateful for your passion for this project. Thank you.

Among my family, friends, and colleagues who supported my pursuit of this creative venture, I am especially thankful for Chas who encouraged me to share this knowledge and accommodated my need to focus on the project. Yet, he was also that instigator of distraction who recognized when I needed a break. Love to you all!

Any errors, omissions, or shortcomings remain my own responsibility.

Disclaimer

This book is intended primarily as a tool for arts administrators, community leaders, self-producing artists, and those who present their own or others' work. As a practical guide, it is full of information, tactics, and strategies that answer *why* and *how* to effectively produce and manage arts initiatives. The strategies described are also relevant for community and municipal political audiences.

The reader can be assured the content of this book does not rely solely on the experience and/or opinions of the author as a professional consultant in arts administration and the arts sector. It is grounded in an evidence-based framework that includes multiple research sources, peer-reviewed research articles, and sector-wide expertise.

No warranty may be created or extended by sales or promotional materials based on this work. The advice and strategies offered in this publication may not be suitable for every situation.

This book is sold with the understanding that the publisher is not engaged in rendering legal, accounting, or other professional services. If professional assistance is required, the services of a competent professional within their area of expertise should be sought. Neither the publisher nor the author shall be liable for damages arising herefrom.

Applying the strategies and tactics presented herein is not a guarantee of success in meeting planned or anticipated outcomes. Every effort has been made to present information that is complete and accurate. This book is to be used as a general guide and not the ultimate source on leveraging the value of and components of the arts ecosystem for programming, partnerships, operational, advocacy, public relations, and community-building achievements.

Should the author choose to provide reference to an organization or website as a citation and/or potential source of additional information, it does not mean the author or publisher endorses information on said organization's website, recommendations provided, or the organization itself. Further to this, readers should be aware that internet websites listed or referenced within this work may have changed or disappeared between the time when this work was written and when read.

If you do not wish to be bound by the above, you may return this book to the publisher for a full refund. Please visit https://www.proctorshiftconsulting.com for details on how to proceed.

Introduction

The arts sector affects us all, cutting across sectors, communities, and societies. Broader awareness of how artistic presence intersects these areas fosters understanding of important advantages and benefits realized when partnering with arts sector stakeholders.

The arts are not static. Possibilities to explore and discover unexpected outcomes are infinite. In understanding how and why this is important, we must share our knowledge to not only reach but also expand unexpected outcomes. Whether that be to understand the value of an artist living in your community or to initiate a conversation with an arts administrator that leads to a unique, creative partnership. The options are endless.

This book provides case studies, summaries of benefits, and references to academic documents that support the advocacy work inherent in the role of arts administrators. The reader will also find tools that support administrators in their personal discovery and development of a new narrative for their own partnership development and advocacy efforts. This new narrative incorporates unrealized local resources and assets that benefit the arts ecosystem overall, while acting as a positive lever for individual partners who integrate with arts sector stakeholders.

Anyone can benefit from the knowledge in this book, not just those who work in the arts. If more people working **outside** the arts sector understood how artistic matter inherently affect their local community, the need to write this book would diminish substantially. Arguments to support the arts sector can fall on deaf ears. Decision makers may not grasp the complexity of the arts ecosystem—they may not realize the sheer number of stakeholders their decisions benefit, sway, or limit. These decisions can put into motion immediate and long-term ripple effects that permeate negative value across the arts ecosystem.

This is a mistake.

The arts have proven potential to enhance local, regional, national, or even international prosperity. It is likely businesses, communities, families, or municipalities are already positively affected by artists in their midst. If not, the value of the arts and those who create art should be considered.

This book proposes to lift the veil on subtle but highly influential impacts the arts bring to communities while highlighting how these impacts bind multiple, intersecting sectors and economies. Before the CODIV-19 pandemic, examples of artistic influence were all around us, although not as evident to some or appreciated by as many. However, in the midst of the pandemic as artists, musicians, actors, art galleries and many other artistic sources shared talents and collections through digital media platforms, connection to an artistic presence was felt everywhere. In giving freely to others, coping strategies benefited both the giver and the receiver. Communities came together through fundraising campaigns tied to online concerts, artists shared their talent with neighbours from their outdoor balconies, and large corporations partnered with arts organizations to pay professional artist fees for online concerts—all as our eyes funnelled content from our digital screens during 'shelter in place' orders from public officials.

From a global event such as COVID-19, lessons are learned, priorities shift, and humanity rises to meet every new and life-altering challenge. We have been forced to adapt, almost overnight, to new social norms; 'social distancing' was redefined to 'physical distancing' almost as quickly as it emerged. It became apparent that as public officials asked us to #stayhome, our craving for social connection did not wane, but compelled us to search, find, and share online content that supported each other, human-to-human.

This global event has unexpectedly infused communal lived experience that exemplifies the value of the arts in our everyday lives. Due to an increased level of consciousness associated with the importance of the arts, the need to advocate for the arts may seem less critical at this juncture. Should we assume that a broad hypothesis has been proven, leaving us to wonder, "Are the questions related to artistic value that were posed prior to the COVID-19 pandemic now relevant?"

They are. And this book will help to answer *how* and *why*.

The Arts Ecosystem

The arts ecosystem is a complex arrangement of creativity, artistic development, idea generation, business, contracts, funding models, funders, artists, presentation venues, and reams of individuals in multi-faceted roles. To guide your understanding of the arts ecosystem, I conceptualized the ecosystem as the context for inter-related, artistic creative flow and influence among three entities: Artists, Arts Sector Intermediaries, and Creative Industries. The vying interests and intentions that occur among stakeholders within these entities can appear as polar opposites:

- artistic expression versus revenue generation
- ever-changing creative output versus stable return on investment
- meagre resources versus industry-led productions with large budgets
- social impact versus quantitative financial reporting (return on investment)
- working in a home studio versus working on a sound stage.

Comparisons of artistic creation with economic development or societal value are complex. However, numerous collaborations emerge from within the multiple layers and sectors, often among artists or between arts sector intermediaries such as venues or galleries. Sometimes collaborative outputs that flow through intermediaries reach scalable production and commercial success. Several factors determine who or what finds success at industry levels, yet neither the process nor a creative intention guarantees success. It is a non-linear path that eludes many artists.

Lack of commercial success does not equate to lack of talent nor decreased value an artist holds at the local level. Consistently, superb artistic talent is honed in the studio, at the writing desk, and increasingly on a computer. Artists' output actually drives the arts sector and arms-length industries, particularly at the local level. Entire communities benefit socially, intellectually, emotionally, and economically from artists' presence and creative output. Artists' creative capital benefits many stakeholders (knowingly or unknowingly) who, either assertively or passively, come to expect the benefits of a vibrant arts community.

Many terms are used to describe the arts sector, artists, and the variety of disciplines within which they work. Some commonly encountered terms and their synonyms are:

- Cultural sector or arts and cultural sector
- Cultural industries or arts and cultural industries
- Creative economy or creative cultural economy
- Creative industries or creative cultural industries

The intermingling of similar terms makes it a challenge to understand what each term refers to. You are left to wonder what exactly the groups of terms represent and who the stakeholders are. Unclear definitions result in uncertainty of impact, opportunities, gaps, and muddled notions about a stakeholder's position in the larger scope of arts and cultural frameworks. The word *culture* has many meanings to where it practically requires a definition to ensure clarity each time it is used.

Throughout this book, I avoid using the word *culture* or *cultural* without additional identifiers. I chose specific language so readers working within the sector, or those with limited knowledge of the arts ecosystem, will gain equally from the insights.

This book addresses:

- Who is an arts ecosystem stakeholder?

- Where do stakeholders intersect to achieve mutually beneficial outcomes?
- How does a community benefit when artists live and work there?
- How do artists both influence and impact non-arts-centric local sectors and society?
- Why should non-arts-centric organizations and the business community consider building partnerships with artists and the arts sector?

Further, this book focuses on the influence artistry has in promoting prosperity at the local level. Supporting creativity at this level not only supports local community but also broadens opportunities for success for a greater number of stakeholders including (but not restricted to) artists. Trusted, effective partnerships are critical to the process.

How to Read This Book

Leverage the Arts Ecosystem to Influence Local Prosperity is divided into two parts:

- Part 1 describes who the stakeholders are and their impact in the larger ecosystem.
- Part 2 outlines connections between stakeholders and applies practical tools to develop multi-sector, partnership strategies. The principles described in this section are drawn from case studies and lived experience, while the tactics presented enable new outcomes to be leveraged in any community. The concepts are based loosely on a community

development framework called Asset-Based Community Development or ABCD.[i]

I explain how artistic initiatives can benefit local stakeholders through social capital, community development, business growth, and corporate social responsibility scenarios. I outline how to develop relationships and partnerships that lead to successful outcomes including specific steps toward short-term and long-term results. I share key aspects of managing successful non-profit operations. I highlight the importance of community partnerships through advocacy, public relations, marketing, and staff engagement.

Strategies and messages provided in this book reflect best practices and time-tested methodologies employed by me and others. Research and practical application come together, presenting tactics easy to digest regardless of your position within the arts ecosystem or outside the arts sector.

You don't **have** to be an arts administrator, artist, or arts sector board member to read this book, but if you are, these time-tested approaches will support you and your organization to leverage your local arts ecosystem for local prosperity.

This publication was in its final editing stages between February and April 2020, the same period when COVID-19 emerged, aggressively and globally. There is no doubt many arts, business, healthcare, and other sector stakeholders will come through this pandemic, while some will not. It will be important as we reset our priorities, post-COVID-19 pandemic, to maintain and develop community-binding relationships and partnerships that support social, economic, and multi-sector regeneration. We are left to wonder how shifting values and priorities experienced during 2020 will frame our approach to mid- and long-term sustainability of the arts sector, perhaps with mindful intent to redesign systems and bottom lines that clearly envision holistic benefits for all.

Background

The Focus Matrix

This book combines applied and academic knowledge and personal experience as a senior arts administrator. When researching my EMBA Signature Project, I discovered multiple connections (or potential relationships) throughout the larger cultural ecosystem. This finding led me to develop *The Focus Matrix*, a chart that captured a bird's eye view of data linkages and allowed for constructive analysis. For example, the matrix highlighted multi-directional benefits that flow between ecosystem stakeholders and overlap at multiple points. It became clear that *artistic drivers* acted as the foundation of the larger arts ecosystem, benefiting multiple entities who both supported and/or leveraged artistic output. A list of *Key Research Findings* from this analysis is available at the end of Chapter Five. *The Focus Matrix* is available for you to peruse, free, on my website www.proctorshiftconsulting.com.

My practical experience as a senior arts administrator brings another perspective to *The Focus Matrix* findings. I have consciously referenced matrix insights when developing strategic plans that seek holistic, targeted results for both venue operations and development projects in the arts sector. Outcomes include positive organizational cultures, public and community activation, creative partnerships that expand facility usage and programming reach, innovative partnerships that support local economies, increased appreciation for the arts, and improved financial results – outcomes of harnessing interests, skills, and assets both internal and external to an arts organization.

My EMBA research project supported a municipal arts and cultural strategic plan for a small urban city with a population of just under 35,000.[ii] Although the City of Charlottetown, Prince Edward Island (PEI), includes a vibrant tourism sector and culinary delights supported by local agricultural and seafood industries, it is relatively small in size and complexity compared to Canadian metropolises like Montreal, Ottawa, Toronto, Calgary, or Vancouver.

Rural Change-Maker Partnerships

Rural and small urban communities can be change-makers unto themselves, supporting arts and cultural initiatives that positively render them individually and collectively significant. These arts initiatives can further benefit economic, social, and humanitarian factors that extend across decades and even generations. Understanding this concept is the first step; taking it to the level of proactive, multi-partner concepts with long-term vision and community support is the next step. This is where concept development thrives. This is achieved through overall planning, financial, in-kind, and volunteer support.

As an example, Charlottetown, PEI is considered a small urban community populated during the working day by an influx of workers who live in the surrounding rural communities. Yet it hosts the Confederation Centre of the Arts, a national arts institution that commemorates our country's founding fathers, recognizing Charlottetown as the birthplace of Canada. For more than five decades, this institution has been integral in presenting arts-focused activities that drive social, community, tourism, and business activities benefiting local sectors and communities.

Developing supportive partnerships often requires unrelenting determination and an emphasis on advocacy. Arts administrators explain, present, and communicate the value of the arts to non-arts-centric decision makers and community builders while continually building a case for the positive impact of creative artistic work. This advocacy takes considerable time but is most gratifying when the work secures champions for the arts sector who truly understand the larger and long-term impacts driven by the arts sector.

It does NOT matter where you are from or where you live; it DOES matter how you strategically work within your environment…to merely exist…or thrive!

Tension Between Creative and Economic Sectors

A tension commonly exists between artistic and economic considerations. What drives an artistic focus is often the polar opposite to what drives a business or industry. Yet each entity benefits from an *artistic dividend* that results from the diverse art forms within societies.[iii]

Potentially conflicting objectives must be considered to develop and manage a healthy balance between artistic and economic sectors within organizational practices. Examples are:

- Expression of artistic values versus mass entertainment economics
- Meet current demand while creatively extending and/or transforming the market
- Build creative systems to support and market cultural products without supressing individual inspiration (i.e. that which underscores the value in the arts ecosystem)

From a sector development perspective, it is imperative for artists, arts administrators, and non-cultural stakeholders to understand the push and pull effect of underlying dynamics and conflicting objectives within the arts ecosystem. Many business owners, government officials, and supporters may not consider the impact of these conflicting pressures when seeking mutually-beneficial partnerships. These factors—along with ever-changing landscapes of creative, technological, and financial pressures—create multiple challenges to developing mutually-beneficial, arts sector partnerships.

An ecological approach concentrates on relationships and patterns within the overall system, showing how careers develop, ideas transfer, money flows, and product and content move, to and fro, around and between the funded, homemade, and commercial subsectors. Culture is an organism not a mechanism; it is much messier and more dynamic than linear models allow.

-      Crossick & Kaszynska (2016)

Understanding the value of arts and culture: The AHRC cultural value project.

Additionally, the arts ecosystem is both fluid and multi-dimensional in its simplest form. Approaching a partnership conversation that educates, builds curiosity, and bridges opportunity is where the sweet spot lies.

Part 1

What You Need to Know About the Arts Ecosystem

1

Peeling Back: Creative Industries and Economic Growth

Over the last number of decades, many urban centers have come to understand the value of investing in the arts to benefit economic gains and long-term tourism or financial outcomes. Generally, arts administrators in urban areas find they are no longer *continually* advocating for the value of the arts to obtain buy-in from decision makers, partners, and funders for initial support. Advocates in many rural and small urban communities must constantly present compelling cases and reasons as to why the arts are important.

Some urban municipalities have transitioned into the next generation of cultural sector development, leveraging the arts sector for community building through inclusion, accessibility, diversity, and improved social well-being.[iv] For example, art galleries and hospitals around the world are partnering to study the benefits and impacts of various arts discipline within the healing process on-site at hospitals.

These benefits are not exclusive to urban centers. They occur naturally because of human interaction with many facets of the arts. However, social outcomes can be far-reaching when the breadth of their impact is realized and adopted in planning and measurement frameworks.

> Whether by providing a sense of belonging through **community**, fostering **empathy** through connection with others, or bringing much needed perspective via a sense of **discovery**, culture has intrinsic, lasting value and is a **force for good** in our changing society. {Emphasis added}
>
> - Business/Arts, Nanos Research, & LaPlaca Cohen (2018)
>
> *Culture Track: Canada*

Having arts sector champions and advocates external to the arts sector is golden. Equally important are champions with knowledge of the social and intellectual benefits the arts provide over and above economic gains. Absent understanding the broader benefits of the arts, a focus on economic gain becomes the primary driver for investment.

An economic focus leverages festivals (e.g., music, ethnic, writers, creative/cultural industry, etc.), tourism (linked closely to festivals) and events. Increases in tourist visits have a ripple effect on revenues for restaurants, hotels, events, galleries, museums, heritage sites, and other local attractions. Everyone benefits...or do they?

What of the livelihood of those who create the works leveraged by creative industries and business sectors? Do artists receive appropriate financial and societal consideration for their individual or collective contribution that attracts attention to a place? Do communities embrace the value of local artists outside of the large festivals and events to which they contribute? Does the community support artists through the local ecosystem of arts organizations, programming, and community building? Are creative talents valued for non-monetary social impacts and compensated appropriately?

Feeding the Creative Value Chain

At this time, the creative industries (film industry, technology industry, publishing industry, television industry, and others) are significant contributors to and supporters of the arts sector. The creative industries might be considered self-sustaining and scalable, based on the provision of return on investment to government, other funding sources, and digital distribution platforms. Who participates at this creative industry level of the ecosystem is often dictated by business outcomes. If there is an acknowledgement toward the rudimentary and foundational components of artistic creation from which creative industries benefit, that can seem secondary to profitability.

If the perceived value of artists or their work is weak, industry-associated money and power will continue to dictate in favour of business as opposed to artistic creation. Absent artistic creative outputs, these same creative industries and the associated economic generation would be null and void, however.

What if artists stopped creating? Then what?

This lack of understanding about the value of the arts is not a new scenario. However, understand the playing field and potential ramifications. The power distance relationship between decision makers and business is often closer (or stronger) than between decision makers and artists/arts administrators.[v] Unfortunately, when those with power and money hold a closer relationship to decision makers, they have more influence than those at the furthest power distance from decision makers.

> **Power distance** is a term that describes how people belonging to a specific culture view power relationships—superior/subordinate relationships—between people, including the degree that people not in power accept that power is spread unequally.
>
> *https://study.com/academy/lesson/hofstedes-power-distance-definition-examples-quiz.html*

The playing field is far from even. Arts sector leaders and administrators continually work to bridge (or narrow) this unrelenting gap. Regardless of advocacy efforts that incorporate academic research to educate decision makers, every effort must be made to build long-term, trusting relationships to help shorten the power gap. Conversations should include subjects and associated research or references that support your goals and reflect arts sector development in your community, ideally focusing on that which benefits multiple stakeholders. For example, should your work positively position civic engagement in the arts, reference Statistics Canada's data on arts participation and data from your venue and your community to give local perspective.

Artists and arts sector intermediaries develop and spur creative content and the value chain, including the larger creative industries. Yet, these same creatives who drive the sector ***do not effectively leverage their own value*** in this power-distance scenario.

Relationships Close the Gap

Governments at all levels (federal, provincial/state, municipal) have made great inroads to ensure the voices of the cultural community are represented in research, fact-finding studies, surveys, and other community-engagement measures. These outreach methods are helpful but do little to reduce the power distance between decision makers and arts/arts administrators. When it comes down to specific policy discussions and decision making, where do policy makers and politicians turn for those trusted relationships and associated conversations off the record?

It remains a common practise that arts sector representation or influence is consistently absent or poorly represented in the decision-making room or at the table. It is critical for decision makers not engulfed in the complexity of the arts sector to build relationships actively and directly with arts administrators and artists. By better understanding the complexity of the ecosystem from which artists make their livelihood, those operating at strategic decision and policy-making levels can clearly consider positive and negative ramifications that impact artists' livelihoods.

> The possible economic benefits flowing from arts and culture are considerable, and so it is in some ways surprising that economic impact, often defined more narrowly than conventionally understood by economists, has become the principal way for proponents of arts and culture to argue its economic importance. Their wider consequences for creativity and innovation in the economy might be more significant but have been the subject of less research. Bruce Seaman's words, as long ago as 1987, remain pertinent: "In a sense [arts proponents] are choosing to play one of their weakest cards, while holding back their aces." (Seaman, 1987, p.280).
>
> - Crossick & Kaszynska (2016)
>
> *Understanding the value of arts and culture: The AHRC cultural value project.*

Otherwise, it's not feasible to expect these decision makers to comprehend or consider the ramifications of their decisions to the artist. This is a critical scenario, especially within legislation, policy, and funding criteria programs.

Uninformed decisions create instability, often setting off negative chain reactions for artists and arts sector intermediaries to navigate. This creates an unbalanced and unstable arts ecosystem and has the potential to lessen creative outputs, dilute the creative process, and undercut the value chain that feeds creative industries. An example would be criteria tied to funding – either for the individual artist or an arts organization. With an artist, their application for funding is often tied to specific criteria their project must consider. 'Ticking the boxes' to meet funding program criteria limits an artist's full scope of creativity that might otherwise be explored and applied. Are we setting up our artists to prioritize imposed criteria that limits their creative output rather than lead the process through work infused with unlimited muse and reflection? Are artists being led rather than leading the creative process?

This situation is not new. However, with growth in creative industries and associated economies, the number of influential stakeholders pressuring government grows too. Many bodies lobby government to represent their own or their partners' benefits. Governments and businesses at all levels are aware of economic development opportunities. Many are eager to leverage arts presentation activities to increase business revenues in their communities.

This is not wrong, but we are at the point where we need to reconsider the innate creative value that artists contribute to preserve the integrity of the sector. When any stakeholder other than the artist or their appointee directs the creation of their work, the full potential of the artist and their creative work is lost. We must earnestly view the sector through a holistic lens that values core artistic creators (artists) as the germ that drives artistic creative content to the arts ecosystem, including creative industry stakeholders.

The creative industries utilize artists' performance and creative content, such as actors and writers—agreed. But who or what is leading the development and production of the film, television, gaming, electronic, and technological integration of creative content? The actors? The artists? Writers? Corporate industry leaders? Government?

> The **non-profit cultural sector contributes research and development for commercial cultural providers**, with public funding enabling them to take risks with creative content and ideas. We nonetheless lack a systematic understanding of the processes that link the different parts of the cultural ecology. [Emphasis added]
>
> -   Crossick & Kaszynska (2016)
>
> *Understanding the value of arts and culture: The AHRC cultural value project.*

Who or what is driving the creative industries? Is there an entity that works in isolation from other entities and intermediaries within the creative sector?

Shifting Paradigms Excluded: The Artist's Right to Copyright

Canadian artists seek to improve Canada's copyright legislation for better recognition of their ownership of original creative artworks and subsequent payment for the use and representation of the works. Final Standing Committee reports were presented to the federal government early in 2019.

But artists and arts sector leaders were not pleased.

Canada's federal government appointed the Department of Innovation, Science and Economic Development (ISED, the department that represented industry) to lead the file. This standing committee sought input from Canada's cultural industries. In response, the Department of Canadian Heritage established a separate committee to consult with the arts sector within a two-year period. Their subsequent report, *Shifting Paradigms*,[vi] captured their findings and recommendations from the arts sector and was presented to the ISED standing committee early in 2019. Astonishingly, not one recommendation from *Shifting Paradigms* was accepted by the ISED standing committee nor included in the Statutory Review of the Copyright Act submitted to the 42nd Parliament, 1st Session by the Standing Committee on Industry, Science and Technology in June 2019!

Arts sector leaders and creatives (artists), those who drive the arts ecosystem, were shut out of the process in the end. Their voice was silenced. The arts sector called *foul*. With arts sector input excluded, the final report presented to government did not represent a balanced, holistic view of the larger arts ecosystem. This scenario speaks loudly to power distance relationships, the focus on economy-driven results, and the dismissal and disregard for the value that artists and arts intermediaries deliver within their own creative intellectual property (IP).

Copyrights protect artists' IP and revenue sources. Copyright includes publishing rights, performance rights, distribution rights, and protection for musicians, authors, visual artists, and others. These rights are often secured at the point of publication, but this is not always the case. The opportunity to redefine the legislation to better protect the rights and livelihood of artists is especially important during this period of disruption and digital transformation. Emerging distribution platforms and digital imaging processes make the need to protect IP that much greater.

Changes to Canada's copyright legislation remain pending following presentation of the Statutory Review of the Copyright Act in 2019. This powerplay undercuts the creative sources that drive the arts ecosystem. Politicians and lobbyists need to understand what is at stake. The sector needs to build stronger partnerships and relationships to make that happen; otherwise, everyone loses.

The Arts Sector Ecosystem

Grasping the inter-related components and overlapping relationships within the arts sector ecosystem is challenging. From a bird's eye view, I provide a figure (below) illustrating how artistic, creative content and its influence flows from the *core artistic creator* to the creative industries. Know artistic content can be tangible or intangible and the path is far from linear, more often than not.

An artist's work is supported by arts organizations (such as arts councils, artist-run centers, professional training, artist-in-residence programs, project funding, and more), presenters/promoters (including galleries, theatres, venues, individuals, and groups), collaborative hub spaces, and any other platform that enhances, workshops, develops, or presents artistic works for public consumption. This component of the ecosystem is referred to below as *arts sector intermediaries.*

The *creative industries* are focused on production and distribution of creative content. Many people think of film and television only; however, they may not consider book publishers, music industry publishers, or graphic design occupations, architectural works, and an increasing number of technology-based creative content.

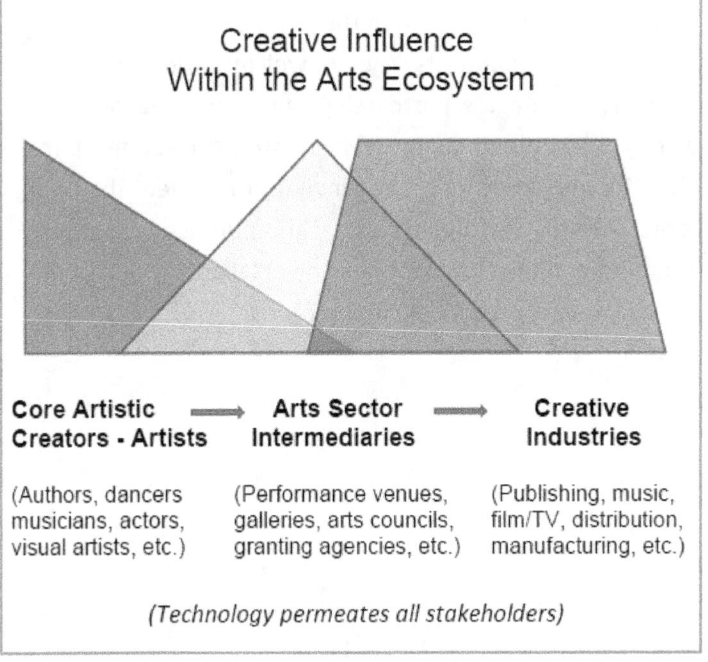

Figure 1: How artistic creativity influences the arts ecosystem; From idea germination to scalable distribution and revenue generation.

Artists, arts sector intermediaries, and non-arts-centric stakeholders (those outside the arts sector) are intrinsically linked at the local level. The non-arts-centric stakeholders are those who can benefit from but are not directly involved with the arts sector as a profession. They would be considered a partner with arts sector intermediaries. It is from this reference point this book focuses on partnerships, advocacy, and community building.

Understanding the arts sector ecosystem at the local level also benefits arts administrators in their day-to-day engagement and development activities. In my experience, it is beneficial to gather information about an artist or their specific works to *understand* their perspective and *why* an artist does what they do. You can then clearly position the purpose of an artist, their role, and associated impacts. You are well informed to plan *what* (such as strategies, partnerships, programming, and advocacy) and implement *how* (such as strategic actions, public relations, sharing knowledge, and invitation) to meet the targets and objectives of your organization. This approach to engagement and development has universal application and is not specific to arts sector development.

- Creative industries provide a linear return on investment (ROI) to government and other funding sources. Their digital distribution platforms are most often dictated by business outcomes.

- The power distance relationship between decision makers and business stakeholders is often closer than power distance relationships between decision makers and arts sector leaders. Relationships with less power distance have more influence.

- Decision makers should recognize those positioned furthest in a power distance relationship—stakeholders at the grass roots level—often shoulder the greatest impact of decisions made.

- It is incumbent upon decision makers who do not have explicit insight to the multi-faceted complexity of the arts sector to build trusted, long-term relationships that consistently utilize arts administrators and artists in policy and programming decision making (besides consultation processes). Value their time appropriately.

- An unbalanced representation of stakeholders, with less input from artists or arts organizations, has the potential to negatively affect creative outputs, dilute artistic creative processes, and undercut the value chain that feeds creative industries.

- Build trusted relationships with grass-roots arts sector stakeholders. Guard against biases toward artists and consider the realities of their often tenuous careers.

- Core artistic creators (artists) are the germ that drives artistic creative content and the arts ecosystem, including that which flows to creative industry stakeholders.

- Artists and arts ecosystem beneficiaries (those outside the arts sector) are intrinsically linked at the local level through their direct or indirect response to emotions and activities both tangible and intangible artwork sets in motion.

- Artistic creative capital benefits all stakeholders (knowingly or unknowingly) within a society that comes to *expect* and appreciate the benefit of a vibrant arts community.

Case Study: River Arts District, Asheville, North Carolina, USA

RE: ARTISTS + BUSINESS + TOURISM PARTNERSHIP = AN ARTS ECOSYSTEM

I visited Asheville, North Carolina, in 2015 while undertaking research for an arts sector/economic development project focused specifically on creative hubs. I was drawn to the River Arts District (RAD), an approximate two-square mile area that housed former warehouses and industrial buildings to the east of the railroad that runs alongside the French Broad River. After more than three decades of artist habitation, the RAD boasted more than 200 artists producing uniquely-styled, discipline-specific, creative works. Products were displayed for purchase in working galleries and studios, where you could often speak with the artist and learn more about their work. Also scattered within the district were restaurants to replenish and refresh visitors/walkers.

I learned this district grew out of necessity. Artists needed low-cost rent and large spaces to produce their works and, in the 1970s, a local property owner rented specifically to artists in the RAD, eventually selling to those who showed the interest and ability toward good stewardship of their building. The trend to provide low-cost rent for artists and offer select property sales to artists (generally one or more artists) continued during the 1980s, 1990s, and onward into the twenty-first century. This practice allowed artists greater control of their expenses (rent and production costs) to counter limiting economic development forces.

The RAD artists have formed a membership organization supported by an associated governance structure and active partnership with local business, tourism, and municipal sectors. The Asheville Convention and Visitors Bureau is the lead organization supporting tourism initiatives and promoting visitation to the RAD. This organization works closely with the Asheville Chamber of Commerce to support the RAD artists, their businesses, and their significant contribution to what makes Asheville 'a wonderful place to visit and live'.

Together, stakeholders discuss challenges, gaps, and opportunities when considering planning and economic development initiatives. They identify positive and negative influences that impact the RAD, other non-RAD contributors to the local arts sector, and ultimately the core artistic creators, the artists. The Chamber has acted as both a facilitator and proponent for arts and cultural development, wishing to preserve the competitive advantage of their arts district/economy and the artists it houses.

Economic development takes on a holistic approach, favouring sustainable artistic practice and arts sector growth. Partners recognize a unique asset in their community and leverage (not exploit) it, benefiting multiple stakeholders (artists, business, tourism) by developing a rooted, local economy over the long-term.

During my visit, some artists informed me that money 'from the north' was threatening building ownership. Artists felt real estate interest from out-of-state buyers would lead to gentrification beyond sustainable means. This is a cycle with (often) negative impacts as some artists—the creators and

anchors of what attracts people and economic growth—are all
but forced to leave that which they have influenced. Without
mindfulness to this cycle, the resulting essence of *place*
transforms into *corporate economic* as opposed to *grass-roots
unique economic*. Keeping (and protecting) artists and their
livelihood safeguards a community's authenticity and shields a
rooted, local economy.

2

Arts Administrators: Hub of the Arts Ecosystem

Arts sector intermediaries manage and drive economic, social, and creative results. Staff and management of these organizations are hardworking arts administrators, often with a holistic view to the big picture. Effective arts administrators recognize four entities of the arts ecosystem: the artists, local arts sector (non-arts-centric) stakeholders, local arts sector intermediaries, and the organizations they are charged with operating. They know how to strategically maneuver between each group of stakeholders. In the process, they gather knowledge and build understanding toward intention, needs, gaps, opportunity, and barriers. At the same time, arts administrators build bridges and partnerships, working in tandem to enable multiple initiatives. It is a multi-faceted, fascinating, exhilarating, challenging, and exhausting role not for the faint of heart!

What is an arts administrator? Many arts administrators are driven by a want (some might say a need) to provide a platform for artists to develop and present their creative works. Perhaps, through their work, they become a change-maker in their community?

Often arts administrators hold a dual role of artistic director. Their career might have evolved through the creative stream of the ecosystem: an artist self-producing their work within singular or multiple artistic disciplines.

Other non-artistic arts administrators possess organizational skillsets (less artistic, more big picture operations and community impact) and a passion for the arts. Anecdotally, they do not possess the same creativity inherent among artists, but they do exhibit, or develop, administrative, fundraising, and marketing skills associated with business ecologies. Post-secondary arts administration courses train for a multitude of responsibilities within the field. These educational pursuits benefit the sector, expanding the capacities and skillsets of early and mid-stage arts administrators. In the reality of the present day, artists also remain actively involved in administration, operations, and presentation activities.

The Value Chain *Germ*

Developing the arts and cultural sector at the local level falls primarily to arts administrators. I say this because they are the connector between artists and other arts sector (non-arts-centric) stakeholders. They build community networks within an ecosystem that intersects under varying conditions. Obtaining buy-in from local stakeholders, many of whom possess only implied or limited knowledge of how the arts sector benefits their community, is a struggle. Even fewer understand the incredible balancing act that arts administrators undertake; this, unfortunately, may also include those to whom administrators report to – their board.

Viewed at arm's length, the cultural sector might seem to thrive, yet, a tremendous pressure to survive (let alone thrive) is ever-present at the root level. The germ of arts sector creative content continues to survive, however. Administrators and artists continue to adapt to the ever-increasing demands of externally-driven content development initiatives.

Accommodation to evolving external requirements either slowly chip away at blue-sky creativity (without boundaries) or limit creative development based on pre-determined criteria (for example, in targets or objectives) to access financial support. Is the system inadvertently swaying artists from their primary role as mirrors of society by limiting their creative options? And what of non-prescriptive creative works that organically grab our attention through unconventional topics and make us think, as opposed to creative works that deliver a semblance of pre-determined results?

In understanding the basis for artistic value and its long-standing role in society, identify the value of who, or what, germinates the sector. Without question, as I have alluded to and based on multiple sources, it is **the artist and their artwork!** The focus on artistic value is a key element to understand for all ecosystem stakeholders. Absent valuing what nurtures and is the bedrock of the ecosystem, the role of artists is well-positioned to diminish or collapse over time, affecting the larger ecosystem. I don't mean to sound too pessimistic here, but after decades of research, studies, and practical evidence, there remains a lack of understanding (and often an erosion) of the value artists contribute to our society. We must move forward, overcoming our fear to engage new models and partners and let go of those that do not complement or serve artistic value. In doing so, we must develop trusting, long-term and mutually beneficial relationships one person and one organization at a time.

We are at a point where the *perception* of artistic value might be changing—highlighted during the COVID-19 global pandemic—but is *respect* for artistic influence shifting at the same pace? The value of art is becoming more closely attributed to social change issues, cross-cutting communities through social and well-being initiatives. We must continue to grow in our understanding and respect for artistic works and their multi-faceted impacts – socially, creatively, economically.

Recognizing Artistic Value

An increasing number of artists are being forced to leave the sector as a means of survival. The leading factor for departure from the sector is unstable and unpredictable incomes, which leads to burnout.[vii]

The present-day reality of surviving as an artist often dictates that many artists generate primary incomes from work *outside of* (and in support of) their artistic practice. This shift in priorities dilutes artists' creative energies and their artistic practice overall. They are creating less![viii] Others have stepped back from their artistic practice due to ever-increasing demands for business and promotional skill development. This situation remains anecdotal at this time but is familiar refrain within arts-centric conversations.

We must also remember those artists whose works are below the radar, so to speak. Perhaps their practice is overlooked due to their senior (50+) years, yet, their discipline-specific expertise is in limited supply or waning within the ecosystem. Perhaps their techniques are considered old by today's standards, but their skills are recognized as invaluable by their peers. Perhaps some artists don't have the technical skills, equipment, or monetary means to actively promote themselves in today's online society. Do we want to consciously discard or turn our backs on people whose skills and catalogues of work are one-of-a-kind? Should we not be taking every opportunity to transfer knowledge from one generation to the next, while embracing unexpected lessons through lived experience in the process?

As the arts ecosystem evolves, we must address deficiencies in capacity and value that undermine the participation of accomplished artists. It is not only the ecosystem but society that will feel the greatest impact.

In understanding artistic value, let's consider what influences an artist's work. Why do artists locate to their chosen municipality? What challenges and benefits do artists seek when moving to or staying in a community? Who and what in the local ecosystem support their work? Detailed insights to these and other benefits[ix] that artists influence are outlined in Chapter 6, *Benefits That Artists Influence.*

Internal Partnerships First!

Board of directors' membership are usually elected and possess a variety of skillsets representing various sectors of their local community. They bring important relationships, knowledge, and links to your community; the importance of their volunteer work aligns (or should) with that of their senior arts administrator(s). Entrusted to lead their organization's strategic planning and development efforts, board members are generally responsible for strategic and visionary leadership and fundraising support within an organization. They hire and entrust day-to-day management and operations decisions to their senior administrator(s), who then reports back to the board.

> Board management and governance were raised repeatedly as areas in pressing need of new approaches and/or support with managing the time and resource burdens. The sector, collectively, wants to advance these skills as a direct response to the value gap and funding shortages it experiences.
>
> - Work in Culture (2019)
>
> *Making it work report: Pathways towards sustainable cultural careers*

When board members' efforts do not align with, or perhaps overstep, management's area of responsibility, well-intentioned efforts can cause more time, effort, and potential harm within operations. Given the already-challenging role of arts administration, where human and financial resources are often squeezed, board members are well-advised not to disrupt (even if unintentionally) the already multi-faceted role of the arts administrator. Working collaboratively while taking cues from your senior administrator ensures fundraising and development initiatives dovetail with operational schedules, promotions, programming, and resources. An internally supportive role that strengthens internal collaboration is foundational for success in every aspect of operations and external partnerships. (Chapter 8 explores *Building Partnerships* in more detail.)

A critical component of a sustained arts sector is collaboration (partnerships) plus programming (artwork). These core components are established at the root level of the arts ecosystem, particularly within arts organizations or through an individual artist. Those that thrive connect internal or solo effort to external support: **excellence in artistic output** *(insert your discipline of choice here)* navigates a **network of advocates** that includes volunteers, philanthropists, community organizations, public funders, and others. These supporters both appreciate and see the value of having an artistic presence in their community.

CHAPTER SUMMARY

- Arts administrators are the connector or link between artists and the larger ecosystem. Community networks intersect through arts organizations under varying conditions.

- Arts administrators know how to strategically manoeuvre between each group of stakeholders. They build understanding of intention, needs, gaps, opportunity, and barriers, bridging to partnerships and working in tandem with stakeholders to enable multiple initiatives.

- Develop trusted, long-term, and mutually beneficial relationships one person and one organization at a time. This is a *must* to leverage the greatest impact over the long term.

- Arts administrators must accommodate evolving requirements within pre-determined targets and objectives to access many forms of financial support. These restrictions chip away at otherwise boundless creativity or development initiatives that lead to organic, unexpected, and often powerful outcomes.

- Arts ecosystem stakeholders should consider how arts activities ultimately generate positive social and economic well-being. They should be mindful of community impacts to activate partnership interest and buy-in.

- In understanding the basis for artistic creation and its long-standing role in society we must recognize who, or what, drives the arts ecosystem. Without question, it is **the artist!**

- Absent being valued as foundational drivers of the arts ecosystem, the role of artists is well-positioned to diminish or collapse over time, affecting all else that is built upon the ecosystem's bedrock.

- Artists' participation is essential to accurately identify deficiencies in the ecosystem's capacity and value as it evolves. As the proponents who create artistic value, artists are directly affected by changing expectations, pressures and several technological, funding, or other obligations imposed by external factors.

- If artists are limited or boxed in through restrictive measures, artistic outcomes are diluted. It is not only the arts ecosystem that will feel the impact but societies, too.

- Board members represent their local community. They link important external relationships and knowledge to an arts organization while collaborating with their arts administrators who should be relied upon for their expertise in operations.

- Critical components of a sustainable arts sector are collaboration (partnerships) plus programming (artwork). These mechanisms are established at the root level of the arts ecosystem, particularly within arts organizations or through an individual artist.

3

The Arts Ecosystem: Understanding Segmentation

Many terms are used to describe the arts sector, artists, and the variety of disciplines within which they work. Commonly encountered terms and synonyms include:

- Cultural sector or arts and cultural sector
- Cultural industries or arts and cultural industries
- Creative economy or creative cultural economy or cultural economy
- Creative industries or creative cultural industries

The intermingling of similar terms makes it a challenge to understand what each term references. You are left to wonder what exactly the groups of terms represent and who are associated stakeholders. Unclear definitions result in uncertain impacts, opportunities, gaps, and muddled notions about an entity's position in the larger scope of the arts and cultural sector, industry, and economy frameworks.

The word *culture* has many meanings to where enhanced definition ensures clarity pertaining to its use. Throughout this book, I use specific language to clarify for readers either working within the arts sector or those with limited knowledge of the arts ecosystem, for each to gain equally from the insights.

Unpacking the layers

The figure in this section, first presented in Chapter 1, illustrates and helps to demystify how creative influences overlap within the arts ecosystem. Combined, all three components represent a significant portion of the *creative economy*, that which generates creative and economic value. The ecosystem entities correspond to a *value chain*, meaning that which adds value to a product, an artist's original creation. The value chain supports moving an artist's idea, words, music, visual works, dance, and so on to a broader audience following research, development, production, and presentation phases. The process and number of steps vary for each artistic discipline and specific conditions within a local arts ecosystem. Initial traction in the marketplace for an artistic creation can bring interest from intermediaries to scale the artwork into an industry format through publication, broadcast, film production, or other forms of expansive public presentation.

Each segment of the larger ecosystem intersects with the other segments in multiple ways. The influence of artistic creation supplies artistic content for other ecosystem intermediaries to build upon; generally, this flows as indicated within the following figure.

Contrary to this illustration, and overall, the ecosystem is not linear. Continuous ebb and flow between and among stakeholders occur at various vertical and horizontal intersections within the ecosystem. What this figure represents is how artistic content is present within all components of the ecosystem. This figure does not capture (to scale) the areas of intersection. For example, a larger group of artists may work directly within creative industries than is outlined below, as indicated by the small triangle at the bottom centre of the figure.

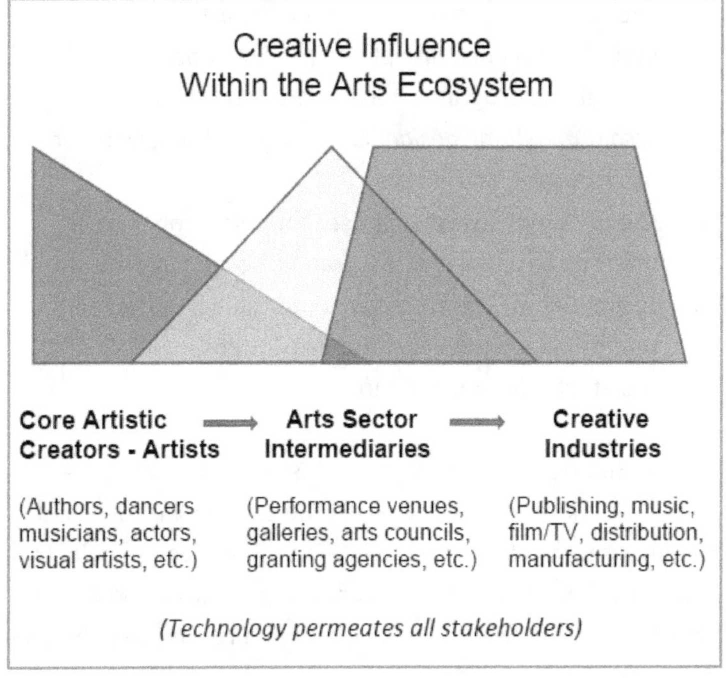

Figure 2: How artistic creativity influences the arts ecosystem; From idea germination to scalable distribution and revenue generation.

Let's break this figure down even further. The components of the arts ecosystem are:

- **Core artistic creators (Artists)**: visual artists, authors, playwrights, musicians, songwriters, dancers/choreographers, actors, comedians, artisans (jewellery, pottery, fabric, woodwork), and more.

- **Arts Sector Intermediaries (arts-centric, local reach)**: arts councils, creative (artistic) hubs, theatres/performance venues, theatre companies, galleries, artist-run centres, festivals, artist workshop and residency programs, community art initiatives/events, discipline-specific schools of study, art training programs, technicians, producers, *fashion/costume designers**, digital technology (ever-increasingly), and others.
- **Creative Industries:** Includes film, television, gaming, internet-based platforms, graphic design, digital technologies, literature/book publishing, music publishing, creative content distribution, architects/design, and more.

Note: * Fashion/costume design is a design-centric, creator-driven occupation that falls between the creative industry and arts-centric sectors. It is often segmented into creative industry occupations; however, I feel the core design focus is more closely aligned to artistic creator output and re-assigned this as an arts sector intermediary.

I have not inserted non-art-centric arts sector stakeholders (local reach) in this figure. They are the multiple stakeholders who reside and exist in your community: residents, municipalities, the business sector, heritage and museum organizations and venues (tangible and intangible), the tourism sector, community groups/centers, other levels of government (provincial/state/federal), philanthropic foundations, and others. These people and entities are often, in various contexts, the beneficiaries of creative content. They will be incorporated into the mix later.

Core Artistic Content

Artists are the idea generators and creators of artistic content produced through stable media (traditional disciplines: painters, dancers, writers, musicians, and more) and other forms of artistic expression. Some forms of artwork transition into next-phase creative development such as theatre workshops, dramaturge and staging, music recording studios, literary editing, or other forms of ongoing development. Artwork might transfer into a digital medium for digital distribution or move directly into presentation spaces such as art galleries or retail spaces. Depending what venues and presentation spaces can accommodate, either limited or expanded opportunities for the work exist.

> There has been growing recognition in recent years that separating arts and culture into neatly separated sectors – such as commercial, third-sector, amateur and subsidised – misses the relationship between them, above all the ways in which the commercial sector is intimately connected to the rest in an ecological system.
>
> -   Crossick & Kaszynska (2016)
>
> *Understanding the value of arts and culture: The AHRC cultural value project*

Generally, artworks might be developed or adapted beyond the creator's original work. This process is more commonly applied in theatre or performance disciplines as opposed to visual art.

The creative content or product could be re-worked into a new or enhanced format for distribution (for example, audio recording, hardcopy print, digital publication, visual print, music festival/tour, film, or TV show) that generates promotion and money for many stakeholders in the value chain (for example, festival producers, publishers, performance arts presenters, galleries, or TV networks).

The creative industries (also described as cultural industries) is where scalable distribution intersects with business and consumerism. At this juncture of the ecosystem, a work (e.g. fringe festival theatre work or book publication) might be redeveloped into theatre-based productions, touring shows, or television or film productions. A case study at the end of this chapter highlights how core artistic content flows from an artist to the larger creative industry component of the ecosystem.

Technological disruption of the arts sector is changing creative outputs. As technology evolves, its application and adaptation influence an increasing number of arts disciplines across the spectrum while new forms of creative works emerge. Technologies are integrating with traditional arts disciplines to enhance or displace well-founded creative elements, such as holograms in theatre or concert presentations or electronic music technology. This evolutionary period in the sector is evidence of increased integration with unstable media as art forms and platforms.

Technology-based platforms are considered unstable media. "We make use of the unstable media, that is, all media which make use of electronic waves and frequencies, such as engines, sound, light, video, computers, and so on. Instability is inherent to these media," said V2_Organization and their *Unstable Media Manifesto*.[x] As the sector evolves, we want to embrace technology but also know its inherent instability. What does this mean for the value of artistic creation over the long term?

Many components within the scope of creative industries work within this space of unstable media. Although the creative industries component of the arts ecosystem is not the focus of this book, it is noted so the reader understands its impact in the context of the larger ecosystem.

Making the Local Connection

How does one expand support for artists at the local level? A primary consideration is appreciating how the presence of artists and the function of arts administrators drive exponential benefits to neighborhoods and generate socio-economic impacts. In other words, what does the work of artists and arts administrators do to positively affect your community? This knowledge is especially useful when engaging with people not involved in the arts and cultural sector.

Neighbors and friends may enjoy passive engagement in theatre, film, music, public art, dance, and other creative works. Members of the general public are often cautious to engage beyond a spectator role because they are not an artist or (perhaps) they presume not to understand the full meaning of an artwork. Many people carry a self-imposed fear, a feeling of being out of place, in an (unfamiliar) arts milieu.

This fear can manifest as a barrier to engagement in the arts. The reasons are varied but often reflect a primary barrier: that of not feeling welcome.[xi] This barrier aligns with a person or community not being modelled ("I am not seeing others like me") either in the crowd or on the stage. This is prevalent among immigrant, racialized, or equity-seeking citizens.

Other self-imposed barriers, regardless of colour or ethnic origin, may include fear of being singled out in a crowd, particularly in rural communities. The potential of drawing attention to oneself may heighten feelings of discomfort. These and other considerations reflect an intentional lack of effort to step outside personal comfort zones.

How can we reduce these barriers? What can we do to make everyone feel welcome?

It takes champions and change-makers from both within and outside the arts sector to demolish these barriers. Through a focus on relationships, we can encourage broader inclusion one person, one invitation, and one event at a time.

Leading Advocacy Initiatives

Arts administrators

Arts administrators are leaders and advocates through their public education, communication, and public relations efforts. They build support and appreciation for artists' work in their community. Arts administrators support creative exploration and address financial requirements while being governed by organizational mandates. They support artists' creative initiatives through funding, community, and partnership channels. They simultaneously support and strike a balance between stakeholders' strategic goals and objectives through their interactions with arts sector stakeholders: artists, staff, organizations, board members, and external partners. Arts administrators function as the *connector* between artists and the larger arts sector ecosystem.

Arts administrators continuously build the case for supporting and developing the arts. Principally, those who directly influence the sector's infrastructure, programs, and cultural policy development are the target of such efforts, notably government and community leaders. Public spending on a vigorous arts sector is often trumped by public infrastructure, health, or educational spending. Sometimes, the apparent immediate results from investment in these or other sectors override the long-term, expansive benefits of investing in the arts sector.

> The cultural sector strives to remain loyal to artistic values, but it must also deal with market economics... Ultimately neither can prevail without destroying of the organization; coexistence is the only option.
>
> -   Lampel, Lant, & Shamsie. (2000)
>
> *Balancing act: Learning from organizing practices in cultural industries*

Community Stakeholders

Taking a long view toward arts sector development considers an all-inclusive, coordinated approach with broad, sustainable impacts. A vibrant arts ecosystem advances vibrant, healthy, socially-integrated communities that benefit humanity overall. Residents and businesses that gain from arts sector impacts are served by the same community leaders and decision makers who support arts sector development.

The broader public may not comprehend that arts sector initiatives activate and attract positive, ripple effects for their businesses and communities. For example, tourism impacts tied to music festivals are highly visible, benefiting governments in tax revenues and local business (restaurants, accommodations, and other events or venues) through direct or spin-off revenues. Engaging youth in art forms (theatre, music and others) is said to increase teamwork, creative thinking and higher learning capacity based on emerging research studies. As an extension of their advocacy role, arts administrators should creatively and strategically promote these ripple effects to broader audiences. These efforts create a platform for discussion while building knowledge and buy-in, similar to reciprocity – knowing that your efforts support others and 'others' support you. As the public learns of these benefits, opportunities to actively leverage long-term benefits through social, economic, and well-being measures emerge. In each case noted, opportunities cultivated through and activated by the arts sector benefit both participants and partners.

Significant support for arts sector development is attached to economic development strategies and subsequent quantifiable results.[xii] It is at this point where return on investment often trumps social benefit for key decision makers. It is at this point where arts sector administrators have one of their greatest challenges: to square the long-term value of creative impact as it intersects the short-term value of financial returns. These values combine to trigger desired outcomes but with differing levels of political, economic, and social returns and importance, depending on the stakeholder. For example, building a reputation as a destination for arts and cultural activity takes years of sustained investment by government and business to stimulate multiple layers of stakeholders in arts, business, education, tourism and more.

Cultural sector activities create positive community dividends for residents and businesses, such as quality of life and well-being. Reciprocal resources such as volunteering, in-kind services or product, and financial contributions directly and indirectly support arts sector sustainability.

When communities share a broad understanding of *the value of the arts* and how this benefits multiple stakeholders, opportunities for partnerships are welcomed. Recognizing these as opportunities to further *stakeholders'* goals and objectives activates mutually beneficial results. An important part of building this value quotient within any partnership is leveraging the arts ecosystem beyond financial impacts to include interactive human and emotional connections.

Using Evidence

Research highlights the importance of stable financial support from business, government, and philanthropic sources to the cultural sector. Case studies, qualitative research, and quantifiable data indicate the positive, long-term community growth that can be achieved due (in part) to a vibrant arts and cultural sector. In 2017, the economic impact of culture GDP (gross domestic product) in Canada was $53.1 billion CAD, more than eight times larger than what was estimated for sports GDP at $6.6 billion CAD in the same period.[xiii]

An important point learned over the course of this research, was the need to help build an understanding of value, respect, and opportunity cost in all aspects of the sector.

- Work in Culture (2019)

Making it work report: Pathways towards sustainable cultural careers

The *Arts + Social Impact Explorer*[xiv] (2019) is an online research tool published by *Americans for the Arts*. The interactive pinwheel compiles and categorizes a large body of evidence on the social impacts of the arts. A summary by Hill Strategies about the report noted "creative placemaking projects positively affect residents' feelings about their neighborhoods." In the social justice section, the fact sheet on community cohesion indicates that "arts participation contributes to social cohesion by reducing isolation, encouraging cooperation, and building community networks."[xv]

These are but two of many resources I share in the reference section of this book and in the *News & Resources* section at my website. Links to articles and websites provide accurate data you can incorporate into your advocacy and fundraising efforts and are a treasure-trove of research findings. Bookmark these sites and refer to them often as new reports and data emerge. Use both quantitative and qualitative data to build upon your personal knowledge. Appropriate use of these data resources gives you credibility and strengthens your position in your advocacy efforts.

Rural Arts Communities

Content in this book leans toward the often neglected rural and small urban arts and cultural sector. Positioning the value of the arts within rural and small urban arts ecosystems remains a struggle for arts administrators, even when positioning the potential impacts of investment in the arts through economic development. It is most beneficial to ecosystem stakeholders (artists, arts organizations, heritage and museums, citizens, governments) when municipalities actively promote their local, creative artistic resources by facilitating and championing their social, economic, and community impacts.

Many large urban centers leverage the arts sector for economic development based on a history of positive results. Interest in next-generation cultural sector development is underway in urban centers. In those locations, the value of arts and culture is viewed through the lenses of community integration, diversity, and inclusion. Appreciation of the arts' impacts on society, equity, and well-being is being integrated into strategic planning and community building across multiple sectors and associated municipal departments.

Regardless of community size or geography, identified stakeholders within the arts ecosystem remain the same. The tactics and strategies in this book apply to local arts ecosystems regardless of geographic location or size.

And there is more good news. The evolution of next-generation cultural sector development can be adapted for rural and small urban communities. These municipalities can integrate community building through the arts with a focus on equity, inclusion, and accessibility. They can maximize lessons learned in large urban milieus to knowingly position the arts as a beneficial lever in their communities.

- The Arts Ecosystem includes: Core Artistic Creators (artists), Intermediaries in arts-centric and non-arts-centric sectors (e.g., theatres, galleries, technology, funders, municipalities, recording studios, producers, and more), and Creative Industries (e.g., film, television, music, book publishers, and more).

- Artistic stakeholders are the idea generators and creators of artistic content produced through stable media (traditional disciplines: painters, dancers, writers, musicians) and other formats.

- The creative industries (cultural industries) is where scalable and broad distribution intersects with business and consumerism.

- Technology-based platforms are considered unstable media. Many areas of creative industries work within this unstable media space.

- Neighbours and friends may enjoy passive engagement in theatre, film, music, public art, dance, and other creative works, but many secretly carry a fear of exclusion or lack confidence to venture into unfamiliar surroundings, beyond a spectator role.

- Case studies, qualitative research, and quantitative data indicate that positive, long-term community growth aligns with a vibrant arts and cultural sector. It takes

champions and change makers from within and outside
the arts sector to reduce these barriers.

- Arts administrators are leaders and advocates through
  their public education, communication, and public
  relations efforts. They act as a hub and connector
  between artists and the larger arts ecosystem.

- A healthy arts ecosystem advances vibrant, healthy,
  socially-integrated communities that benefit society
  overall. Residents and businesses that gain from arts
  sector impacts are served by the same community
  leaders and decision makers who support arts sector
  development.

- A broad understanding among communities of how the
  value of the arts benefits multiple stakeholders expands
  opportunity for successful partnerships.

- Positioning the value of the arts within rural and small
  urban arts ecosystems remains a struggle for arts
  administrators, regardless of evident, positive economic
  developments. All arts ecosystem stakeholders benefit
  when municipalities leverage local, creative artistic
  resources and champion their social, economic, and
  community impacts.

Case Study: Kim's Convenience

RE: FROM AN ARTISTIC IDEA—REJECTED—TO AN INTERNATIONAL TELEVISION DRAMA AWARD

The commercial success of a creative artistic work is often a long-term proposition. Developing the final product includes a creative evolutionary process that involves multiple arts sector intermediaries. But examples of commercial success demonstrate there is no guarantee. Often, similar investments of time and money result in limited success by either creative or financial measures or both.

The acclaimed Canadian television comedy, *Kim's Convenience*, is one of those success stories. The show explores inter-generational tensions between immigrant parents and their Canadian-born children. The story was inspired by playwright Ins Choi's experience growing up in a Korean family in Toronto, Ontario. He developed the storyline as a play in 2010 while attending theatre training at the Soulpepper Academy.

Soulpepper is a not-for-profit theatre company in Toronto, Ontario. Founded and guided by artists, Soulpepper has an integrated mission which includes: industry-leading youth outreach initiatives; the Soulpepper Academy, Canada's only multi-year paid professional training program for theatre artists of all disciplines; and a year-round diverse repertory season. [xvi]

Choi was encouraged to send the play's script to every major Toronto theatre company. Each rejected it. However, the Toronto Fringe Festival's New Play Contest balked the trend.

They not only accepted it, but the play became a standout hit in the 2011 Toronto Fringe Festival!

Since then:

- In January 2012, *Kim's Convenience* premiered at Soulpepper Theatre.
- It sold out and was remounted during 2012 and again in 2013.
- A cross-country touring production kicked off in 2013.
- In 2015, the play was presented at Bluma Appel Theatre, Toronto's St. Lawrence Centre for the Arts.
- In 2016, the show premiered on CBC television, averaging 933,000 viewers per episode.
- In 2017, Soulpepper brought the show to New York City's Off-Broadway.
- In 2018, the show gained an international audience through Netflix.

The series has since won: two Toronto Theatre Critics awards (2012), six Canadian Screen awards (2017, 2018), three Leo Awards (2018), one ACTRA Award (2017), one Alberta Media Production Industries Association Award (2018), and one Seoul International Drama Award (2019).

This case study illustrates how creative development takes time to grow, transform through multiple presentation and development platforms and gain commercial traction. The process requires multiple forms of investment in the creation phases and highlights how return on investment (ROI) is a long game: six years from concept to television launch, plus an additional five years working on the original script. Production companies and distributors play an important part in commercial success, while realizing **they would have had little** content to produce and distribute without the playwright's work and determination along with the Fringe Festival's acceptance of the work.

4

Bridging the Gap: Artists-to-Creative Industries

The figure depicting the *Creative Influence Within the Arts Ecosystem* outlines how the participants intersect. It also suggests overlap between core artistic creators and those working in creative industries are less frequent than between artists and arts sector intermediaries. Fewer opportunities to collaborate is not necessarily intentional, but it forms a disconnect between these parties. Thus, a fracture in the ecosystem exists between core artistic creators and industry, between artists and network executives, between ideation and distribution, and between exposure and financial returns.

Often, the skillsets and intentions displayed by artists and arts ecosystem stakeholders are polar opposites, as noted. For example, an artist applies creative visioning and skill to express an image or message for public reflection; a business owner applies business principles to serve their community with a service or a product to generate revenue. Yet, each ecosystem participant desires creative content or perhaps creative applications that link to monetary gain and reflect value for their work. The value attributed to either artistic content or revenue generation depends on each participant's vantage point, including who they serve. If you are investing artistic skills, creative output is your priority; if managing production and distribution of creative content, revenue generation is often your priority.

Arts administrators, and to some degree artists who develop and present new works, can struggle to monetize their ideas, artwork, or programming when their work is not yet proven as a money-maker. It is a longshot that a new artistic work will be a definite money-maker. It is, after all, a new (unproven) piece of work!

Gaining Cross-Sectoral Support

An important component in the mix of creation, cost, and presentation is finding partners to support the process. Gaining support from outside the cultural sector is not out of reach and, in fact, is closer than some may think.

> Cultural industry products evoke intensely private experiences... for the most part they bank on the successful use of creativity, which is a resource that ultimately cannot be controlled.
>
> - Lampel, Lant, & Shamsie (2000)
>
> *Balancing act: Learning from organizing practices in cultural industries*

Understandably, apprehension is a significant factor when venturing into unfamiliar territory. Approaching people who use unfamiliar, sector-specific terms (jargon), measurements, and expectations than those used in the non-profit arts sector can be intimidating. You may wonder, "Do the people I am about to approach appreciate, let alone understand, the arts?" And from there, where do you start?

Arts administrators are familiar with grants, sponsorships, donations, and ticket sales as potential revenue sources. But the path is not always clear when determining how to foster relationships that dovetail financial and non-financial support required to produce new or existing creative works. For example, in *Making It Work—Pathways Toward Sustainable Cultural Careers,* roundtables[xvii] respondents described "a desire to learn how to forge/foster stronger partnerships outside of the culture sector." Another important finding that weighed heavily on roundtable participants was, "The challenge of how to communicate the value of cultural products and experiences as something 'worth paying for'."

What's in It for Them?

By initiating conversations that illustrate value for all stakeholders, arts administrators accelerate buy-in. Framing this conversation around unique assets and a *value proposition* is where you start. A value proposition is based on a unique benefit either you offer, or your partner gains, based on resources, assets, intentions, targets, or objectives that each contributor offers.

Conversations with potential partners present an ideal opportunity for arts administrators to develop shared understanding of value, respect, and opportunity cost[xviii] between their organization and community/business stakeholders. Think of your conversation as an opportunity to educate someone who does not work in the arts sector. This approach offers greater opportunity to develop mutual interests. It is not a *pitch* such as made by an entrepreneur seeking investment in a business idea, although your objective is similar. As an arts administrator, you want to approach the conversation as *an invitation* to support "X" as opposed to *an ask* to support "X".

> Those who donate to culture are motivated by one key factor: Social Impact...
>
> - Of the organization = 77%
> - Of the community = 68%
> - Of the world = 56%
>
> - Business/Arts, Nanos Research, & LaPlaca Cohen (2018)
>
> *Culture Track: Canada*

Your objective is to stimulate curiosity.

Consider sharing information that builds interest in your organization, how it delivers on its mandate, or perhaps explains existing collaborations with artists and their works. Think from another's perspective, someone who knows little about the sector. Perhaps they hold self-imposed barriers to participation? Consider what curiosities or interests they might have.

When exploring an opportunity to collaborate, propose *how* and *why* a particular initiative might be valuable to them. *What's in*

It for Them (a twist on a commonly-cited sales principle: *What's In It For Me* = WIIFM). You are engaging from a new perspective: **repositioning value for the potential partner**. Propose how THEY will benefit, as opposed to how YOU benefit as the artist or arts organization.

Using this method, you invite your potential partner to participate in a more deeply-engaged conversation where you learn about them and they about you. You are establishing a foothold to develop a trusted relationship.

I provide a guide to prepare for these conversations in Chapter 8. For now, understand the importance of positioning your conversation from a different perspective. Do some research to determine if a person or organization is a good fit for your organization. Consider potential benefits and assets each partner might contribute. Prepare these in a list as potential talking points.

Be prepared to also outline the benefits to you, your organization, and/or the artist. Use this opportunity to highlight the value your organization brings to the community and specific societal outcomes you know they value. You have done your research, right?

Unfortunately, rejection is also a reality in this dance. However, your focus is on deepening your knowledge of and relationship with your dance partner. When discovering shared connections, build upon these curiosities to benefit the other organization while introducing a connection to the arts![xix] Be creative. If you raise your potential partner's curiosity about your organization or specific areas of programming, you have established a strong starting position.

Maybe the potential partner is a small business never approached for a partnership before your conversation. Perhaps they fall into the categories outlined below.

Maybe they have never been asked to engage in an arts and cultural initiative. Your conversation might be a unique opportunity that invites entrance into a world unknown to them. You may be opening a new door of opportunity they enthusiastically embrace!

Reasons for Non-Support of Arts and Cultural Organizations (small and medium-sized business)

In all, 65% of small and 52% of medium-sized businesses do not support arts or cultural organizations. When reasons for this are explored, a number of interesting factors emerge including a lack of benefit, interest, or connection with the arts.

In the case of small businesses, the second most frequently-cited reason was simply that the company has never been asked. The fact that so many organizations cite 'not being asked' as a reason for their non-support points up the need for arts organizations to reach out to smaller and medium sized businesses.

-       Business for the Arts & The Strategic Council (2015)

Building the case for business support of the arts

Artists Play the Long Game

When artists create, they are generating tangible or intangible product from an idea, an influence, or a muse. They are expressing themselves and their ideas through their chosen discipline and are (generally) not paid for this creation stage, unless working on a project commissioned or funded through either government or philanthropic sources.

Let's envision a separate creative occupation: the laboratory scientist.

When thinking of medical or scientific labs, we think of chemists, biologists, technologists, or other scientific professionals. Their research discoveries include medical cures, new technologies, and scientific findings that may make a positive impact on society. Scientists spend relentless hours adapting, layering, configuring, and reconfiguring processes, chemicals, or microscopic organisms to achieve desired results.

Overall, scientific research is a multi-faceted trial-and-error process of hypothesis testing. It is safe to suggest that multiple trials and attempts achieve specific results, some taking years or even decades to achieve. Once identified, a successful product deemed to have commercial value enters a new process: that of supply chain management and scalable production into the marketplace. At this point the product is intended (expected) to generate money, providing a return on investment for those who invested in the research process.

The process is a risky, non-linear undertaking. Like any new scientific invention, there is no guarantee of financial (market) success.

Artistic Labs

How does an artist's studio and their tangible or intangible artistic output compare to a scientific lab scenario? Similarly, relentless hours of thought processes, layering, texturizing, and overlaying of multiple mediums occur. For authors, chapters of words are written, edited, thrown out, and the process restarts. For songwriters, melodies and words are constructed into lyrics and chords, with many options not making the final cut. The tone, intent, and creative force of the artist emerges. Regardless of the tools used, the artistic intent is to express something: a story, an idea, a reflection, an interpretation of the artistic creator.

From this short comparison, we see that artists are inventors, too. Granted, their tools and input sources differ from those common to scientific endeavors, but the process is similar. Likewise, artistic creations (and skillful expertise) can take years to develop with no guarantee of financial payoff, while some artworks generate initial interest or impact and find their way into the supply chain and larger marketplace.

Art also aligns with positive social impact, specifically influencing wellness and community development. An ever-growing body of research indicates culturally-charged and culturally-engaged societies support a high well-being index. But this is where our example separates.

The Arts' Impact on Society

Participation in the arts has shown to improve individual cognitive and social well-being. Studying the arts, particularly in primary and secondary school environments, contributes to development of soft skills in areas such as creative thinking, tolerance, well-being, problem solving, emotional intelligence, and team building. In adult years, these skills are highly valued by employers. Many students with a background in arts education become productive, creative employees in ventures outside of the arts ecosystem.[xx]

Canadian business (survey respondents) believe the arts can produce social benefits, such as:

• 82% believe engagement with the arts leads to good health and well-being
• 88% believe youth engagement with the arts helps reduce youth crime and alienation
• 95% say arts education assists in the intellectual development of children

Business for the Arts & The Strategic Council (2015)

Building the case for business support of the arts

Yes, an artist's purpose is to create, but their impact is also psychological and intellectual. We generally agree that introspective explorations of self, society, and the future are cause for reflection and contemplation. Artists have a unique talent to generate creative works that express this reflection and contemplation. Their work both challenges and validates how we think about our world, our communities, and our futures. Artists portray interactions, potential outcomes, historical contexts, and numerous other insights drawn from their artistic creative visions.

What we, the public, see as a creative work is generally not an artist's first attempt to develop their idea. Like a lab scientist, an artist applies multiple combinations and layers of ideas, storylines, workshops, music, colours, and movement, depending on the discipline in which they work, before presenting their final creation.

The popularity of an artistic work is generally based on a social (or critical artistic) response to it. Some pieces are complete when they leave the artists' studios; others require development of ideas, presentation, and technical applications, particularly in performance art. Some art pieces are closely tied to a specific, authentic connection to the place where they were created and that local affiliation contributes to their popularity. Other pieces become popular over time, often with creative economy stakeholders driving their popularity (e.g. marketing campaigns, promotions, festivals, tourism incentives, and others).

Artists and Artistic Value

To a significant degree, we expect artists to entertain us. We enthusiastically express outward appreciation or perhaps feel joy and contentment in response to a creative work, but the *entertainment value* of an artwork is (generally) **not the primary focus of an artist**.

Artists approach their creative intentions through numerous disciplines, often with two distinct intentions. Some artists are *creators,* drawing inspiration from personal ideas, perceptions and environments, dovetailing their processes and means of expression through a chosen art form. Other artists are *interpreters*, meaning an artist who interprets rather than develops an original idea (e.g., developing multiple copies of the same product, albeit with variations in colour or materials; or a person who recreates a painting from a sample model, say in a public painting workshop).

> *Author's Note*: I mention the difference between *creators* and *interpreters* to position original artworks and their value proposition as my intended reference to an artist. Within the context of this book, the research findings presented refer to the *creator* artist as opposed to the *interpreter* artist.

An artist creates because they must. Rarely are they driven by material wealth or fame; rather, they are sharing stories and insights through their chosen medium. This is highlighted through the comparison of the expression of artistic values versus mass entertainment economics.[xxi] This does not mean an artist's work is not valuable nor does it mean they should not be paid fairly for their work. However, it has become common practice to ask artists to donate their artwork, musical talent, and other types of creative output to organized public activities to attract attention and build content for a presenter or another benefactor.

Yet are artists and their work ignored in the larger creative economy in their role as the drivers of content creation? In fact, to recognize artists as critical drivers of the larger creative economy is to recognize that our society would be dismally lacking without them: no music, no films, no books, no dance, no theatre, no (artistic) video content, no pictures, and so much more (or rather, less).

> For cultural consumers, the top three characteristics of their ideal experience are "social," "lively," and "interactive"—indicating that a "fun" cultural experience is, at its core, participatory, dynamic, and rich in social connection.
>
> - Business/Arts, Nanos Research, & LaPlaca Cohen (2018)
>
> *Culture Track: Canada*

And what would become of content sharing on the internet? A multitude of digital platforms would be built to share '…'. What fills in the blank?

Or perhaps these platforms would not exist at all – or at least not in their present form.

Showing appreciation for and understanding the *value* of an artist's work has often translated into utilizing the artist's work for another's agenda as opposed to valuing the work for what it is and what it represents. Those who are entertained by, consume, participate in, learn from, and benefit from the influence of an artist's creativity need to appreciate this fact.

Let me repeat that.

As a society, we must value artistic work for what it is and what it represents in the human condition. What meaning does a special song have between people when marking feelings at a special occasion, like a wedding day? Many public artworks represent historical or local significance, often generating pride or awe within a spectator. Art generates feelings, emotions, and psychological shifts in each of us. We learn. We grow. We all benefit, whether we realize it consciously or not. Those benefits have significant worth.

Perceived Value / Actual Value

An ever-increasing number of intermediaries are claiming space within the value chain of the arts ecosystem, and many of these intermediaries gain revenues related to the presentation and distribution of creative content. These ecosystem participants are not expected to donate their professional work 'for their own exposure' nor to undertake their work without an expectation of payment!

So why should the same be asked of artists?

Many people have genuine intentions to support artists. More important, these supporters must also recognize an artist acts as the germ from which creative industries grow. Respecting the core value of artists is more important than ever during our current historical period of disruption, transformation, integration, and evolution of creative works. With the evolution of changing and integrating forces, we must be mindful of the germ, the origin of creative works.

Compensation and financial value for art and other creative works varies wildly. As occurs in most capital markets, supply and demand are significant factors. Specific value can be predicated upon the discipline-specific artwork presented and the *perceived value* of this work (e.g., a classical musician versus a singer-songwriter; a ballet dancer versus a contemporary dancer). This truth holds whether the presentation is in a theatre, on a sidewalk, in a park, or if the work is presented as a book, on an album (LP), via a digital download, in a frame, as a sculpture, or another art form.

Regardless of the presentation platform, factors of time, place, and connection to targeted and secondary audiences drive pathways to popularity and market success. Financial outcomes are tied to forces beyond the artist's control, many of which are tied to place, distribution portholes, creative industries stakeholders, or creative economy market forces.

Creative 'Germs' Are Withering

To better support artistic creators, financial and business models need to be discussed, evaluated, and reconstructed. A current, growing financial reality for many well-known artists is a widening gap between an expanded public profile and increased consumption of their work versus decreased financial returns. A recent example highlights shrinking revenue streams for musicians,[xxii] even though digital platforms have increased opportunity for distribution of their work. The voice from within the sector is alarmed and getting louder. A growing number of examples illustrate the too-common phenomenon of pennies or fractions of cents as payment (to artists) for thousands of download distribution 'sales.'

All stakeholders within the arts ecosystem, and particularly those stakeholders who benefit from the ecosystem, need to be aware of the critical and worsening financial position for artists. Their very survival depends on the current state of affairs squared with what we, consumers and benefactors of art, want to do about it. If we want to keep our artists working, we need to actively support their creative efforts: first, by active engagement and, second, by improved investment frameworks that drive increased revenues.

These revenues are rightly due into the hands of the artist. This is *NOT* a handout. This is valuing artists and their work in our economy and our society, as essential to our humanity.

Serious consideration must be given to taking a holistic or *balanced scorecard* [1]approach to direct (or redirect) earned revenues back to the artist, the creator of the work. Payment of consultation fees, royalty fees (payment for use), honoraria for

---

[1] A balanced scorecard is a strategic management performance metric used to identify and improve various internal business functions and their resulting external outcomes. Balanced scorecards are used to measure and provide feedback to organizations. *Investopedia (2020)*

policy development input, commissions, or equitable leverage established within copyright acts, globally, are notable opportunities by which the artist can—and should—be supported.

Are there investors lining up to take a chance on what artists are developing 'in the lab' (aka studio)? If not, how can we link individual and corporate philanthropists willing to support creative work but whose hands are tied by government legislation? Let's have government negotiate fair payment by large corporations to compensate appropriately the creators from whose work they benefit. Let's have creative industry stakeholders and corporations offer value for (human) artistic works. Our political leaders could also reconsider charitable tax legislation that prevents or constricts philanthropic giving to non-profit, social enterprise, and charitable organizations that seek to expand their communities' creative, economic, and social impacts.

Outside of creative industry contexts, is it the expectation of funders and philanthropists for artists' work to follow a similar supply-chain-to-market path as (say) the retail sector? Depending on an individual artist, the answer varies widely! Does the artist have a track record of creative or financial success? And even if they do, there is no guarantee of replicating past success. What discipline is being addressed? Ballet? Music? Visual art? Indigenous art? Literary arts? Something else? It must be recognized that some disciplines or artistic approaches do not deliver high return on investment, therefore are not as appealing to investors.

The splintering of equal support across all disciplines of the arts is often driven by return on investment, especially when working in the creative industries sphere of the ecosystem. Potential returns are a risky bet for both artists and scientists. Does this mean we stop creating or stop supporting those who do create? If not for the greater good of humanity, then for what reason should we support artists?

Consider the outcomes if we fail to surpass value-for-work perceptions for artists; the absence of artists and their impacts will be felt across numerous sectors and economies. Without the author, painter, musician, playwright, or other artists, there would not be creative work to distribute, sell, redevelop for television, make into films, build a tourism industry on, present at a festival, or build an industry that supports restaurants, hotels, technicians, designers, and so on. This says nothing of the intellectual, creative thinking, medical correlations, community building, or youth-oriented impacts.

The case study that follows at the end of this chapter is an excellent example of how one writer's creative idea has driven multiple sectors and economies—locally, provincially, and globally—for generations. Consider what the absence of the writer's impact would have been; such a scenario is incomprehensible.

Outside of this case study, the absence of artistic impacts across the entire arts ecosystem is equally inconceivable. To pretend this emerging reality is not at work makes for a slippery slope for artists in a social, economic, and cultural system that continually undercuts a sustainable existence for artists. Without the creators fundamentally developing and feeding the ecosystem, negative impacts across sectors and societies are unavoidable.

CHAPTER SUMMARY

- Anecdotally, overlap between core artistic creators (artists) and those working in creative industries is less frequent than intersectionality between artists and arts sector intermediaries, or creative industry stakeholders and arts sector intermediaries.

- Fractures in the ecosystem exist between creatives and industry and between artists and business executives/owners, as associated by divergent intentions.

- An important component in the mix of creation, cost, and presentation is finding partners to support the creative process when return on investment is precarious.

- Conversations about potential partnerships present an ideal opportunity for arts administrators to develop shared understanding of value, respect, and opportunity cost between their organization and community/business stakeholders.

- When exploring an opportunity to collaborate, propose *how* and *why* a particular initiative might be valuable to them: What's in It for Them (WIIFT).

- Use a conversation as an opportunity to educate those who does not work in the arts sector – position the work of artists and arts organizations as an invitation to participate.

- Fifty-seven percent of businesses that don't invest in the arts have never been asked. The odds are in your favour to ask.

- Artists are inventors. Their labour benefits society but does not guarantee a financial payoff.

- Participation in the arts, regardless of a specific artwork's market success, has shown to improve individual cognitive and social well-being, and influence community wellness and community development.

- The entertainment value of an artwork is (generally) not the primary focus of an artist! More often than not their work is tied to a story, a message, a vision.

- Recognizing artists as critical drivers of the larger creative economy is recognizing our society would be dismally lacking without their artistic input (and output): no music, no actors, no books, no dancers, no theatre, no mirror on society, and so much more (or less).

- Respecting the core value of artists is more important than ever during this historical period of disruption, transformation, integration, and evolution of creative works, including before, during, and after the COVID-19 pandemic.

- There is a critical need to redesign financial and business models to better support artistic creators, arts organizations, and the non-profit sector overall.

- Political and business leaders must consider how to address a holistic approach that redirects an equitable portion of industry earned revenues back to artists to appropriately compensate them, when earnings are gained directly or indirectly from their artwork.

- If we fail to surpass value-for-work perceptions for artists, their absence and subsequent impacts will be felt across numerous sectors and economies.

Case Study: *Anne of Green Gables* by Lucy Maud Montgomery

RE: FROM AN AUTHOR'S NOVEL—REJECTED—TO DRIVING A THRIVING TOURISM INDUSTRY

In 1908, Lucy Maud Montgomery was a published author with the release of her book *Anne of Green Gables,* one of many publications by this now famous, internationally renowned author. Fast forward 57 years and her story is reimagined into a musical theatre production in the capital city of the province in which the book was conceived: Charlottetown, Prince Edward Island. The story told is of a poor orphan girl, familiar with rejection, who was shuffled between multiple families before coming to live with the Cuthbert's on their farm, Green Gables.

Anne of Green Gables—The Musical remains the anchor production of The Charlottetown Festival more than 50 years after its premiere on July 27, 1965. Many commercial and artistic offshoots have sprung from the story's popularity including movie adaptations; numerous museums, including the author's residence, a post office, and an interpretive centre; numerous retail products incorporating branded red braids and straw hat symbolic of the story's heroine, Anne; summer cottage businesses; branded food items; a golf course; and many other tourism attractions. All these activities contribute significantly to Canada's smallest province's economy on a small island that boasts a population of 155,241 residents (Statistics Canada 2019).

The evolution of this once-rejected manuscript into a creative and commercial success that now sprawls across economies and global geographies signifies the potential power of one person's, one artist's, creativity. The artist wrote a simple story embedded in a specific geographic location that captured the imagination of the world.

Creative and economic by-products take advantage of inherent connections audiences have to the story and the place. Adaptations of the published story form how playwrights, producers, film makers, and others working within creative industries shape, scale, and redistribute the story for new audiences and associated platforms. All the while, tourism and arts and cultural industry stakeholders benefit, locally, from global audiences the story attracts.

This...based on a fictional character and a beautiful place, created by an artist from the germ of an idea! **What value should we attach to that?!**

5

Artists: Primary Drivers of the Arts Ecosystem

This section moves into the results of academic analyses. I know, that sounds dry! But really, this information is interesting and helpful. I've presented it in many bite-sized pieces of information to help you discover or deepen your connection to the arts ecosystem where you live.

The research findings discussed in this chapter are drawn from *The Focus Matrix,* an analysis tool I developed when preparing my EMBA Signature Project (a thesis project).[xxiii] The matrix is available for your reference, for free, on my website www.proctorshiftconsulting.com at the *My Book* page under *Support Materials & Resources*. In my research, I discovered key drivers and linkages that influence arts and cultural sector development. I captured these findings through a cross-axis of six *Artistic Drivers* (a seventh is briefly mentioned in the chapter) and a vertical axis of seven *Arts Ecosystem Stakeholders* (the artist is the principal stakeholder) that are found within the arts ecosystem. Don't worry: I lay this information out in an easy-to-read format so you can readily apply these findings to your scope of work within the arts ecosystem.

The benefits artists bring to a community vary in nature and scope, depending on specific conditions and stakeholders within the local environment. Certain conditions make it attractive for artists to live and create in a particular location. Mostly the conditions are practical, but conditions must also support creative development and attract local interest in their work and/or its distribution. These conditions are *artistic drivers.* They underscore artists' ability to live, make money, survive, and have the freedom to create.

Six Artistic Drivers

Six primary **artistic drivers** support the **principal stakeholder, the artist,** to live and work in a specific location. This list of conditions supports an artist's pursuit of a creative art-making career tied to their local community. Artists are one of seven stakeholders but establish themselves as the principal stakeholder given they ignite the larger ecosystem. Outlined below are the primary artistic drivers with short descriptions giving added context.

1) Creative works (including the tools, supplies, and overall environment to create artworks)
2) Place (geographic attraction or features of a place that appeal to artists)
3) Linkages to traditional and non-traditional arts ecosystem stakeholders (providing a support system of art sector intermediaries)
4) Non-financial resources (considering local resources and assets that support artistic creation and presentation, over and above monetary revenues)
5) Visioning (a conducive environment that allows for and supports artistic contemplation, reflection, and broad-based or future visioning)
6) Economics (the opportunity to present, sell, and distribute their artwork)

Combinations of these primary artistic drivers creates an environment to establish a well-supported arts and cultural ecosystem. Although not explicitly stated, artists thrive where these conditions attract other artists and like-minded individuals. The larger an artistic cluster, the larger impact artists will have in your community.

Seven Stakeholders

The artistic drivers have intersecting relationships with seven **arts ecosystem stakeholders**. Generally, stakeholder relationships are in close proximity to artists. Looking through a window of opportunity from a reverse position, non-artistic stakeholders can easily access and connect with artists or arts organizations. Once established, these relationships can benefit individuals, businesses, staff, and broader communities in multiple ways.

The seven arts ecosystem stakeholders are:

1) Artists (principal stakeholders of the ecosystem)
2) Arts organizations (service organizations/presentation venues)
3) Heritage and museum organizations and properties
4) Residents (includes community organizations)
5) Municipality (government)
6) Business (including individuals and service organizations)
7) Provincial/state government

Author's Note: An important eighth stakeholder in Canada is the federal government and associated funding agencies. Although not highlighted in this list, they play an important role in funding the Canadian arts ecosystem through numerous programs and channels. Partnership opportunities and outcomes from national funding sources closely align with information outlined under *provincial/state government* stakeholders.

How do various arts ecosystem stakeholders interconnect? Which stakeholders work best together? Is there a greater impact when specific combinations of stakeholders work together?

The answer is, "The combinations are endless" and "It depends."

To help identify how these relationships and potential outcomes intertwine within your community, consider what resources and partnerships are available to you. What defines current and untapped partnership opportunities? Do you have professional relationships with organizational leaders and other ecosystem stakeholders?

If not, don't worry. Chapter 8, *Your Unique Assets*, walks you through a process to determine who might be a potential fit as a new partner. I also provide helpful tips to prepare you for a first introduction.

These arts ecosystem stakeholders exist in both urban and rural communities. Their existence has influenced relocation factors for both people and business. Generally, personal and professional relocation opportunities weigh quality of life factors often associated with a vibrant arts sector, artistic clusters, and various opportunities to engage in creative activities.

Key Research Findings: Developing A Vibrant Arts Ecosystem

The research I conducted for my EMBA Signature Project revealed the factors that emerged are within an individual arts organization's sphere of development. These factors extend to larger partnership or sector-wide initiatives that include community and municipal development. Consider these findings from multiple perspectives in your strategic, research, and presentation objectives. These findings can support more than one stakeholder in strategic planning, promotional, and partnerships initiatives. They are sub-grouped under three relevant *considerations* when developing a vibrant arts ecosystem, locally.

Developing a vibrant arts ecosystem: An evidence-based approach

<table>
<tr><td colspan="3">Consideration #1: Holistic awareness and development of unique local assets</td></tr>
<tr><td></td><td colspan="2">Authenticity (very important)</td></tr>
<tr><td></td><td></td><td>
<ul>
<li>Be true to place and people yet allow for contemporary creativity that emerges.</li>
<li>Incorporate grass roots/genuine components specific to your locale in ALL initiatives.</li>
<li>Take a risk to be different and apply new concepts.</li>
<li>Do not employ cookie-cutter template applications or solely apply best practices as solutions or initiatives; consider local context and factors for the latter.</li>
</ul>
</td></tr>
<tr><td></td><td colspan="2">Partnerships</td></tr>
<tr><td></td><td></td><td>
<ul>
<li>Harness and take advantage of local expertise, assets, stories, and established outcomes within your community.</li>
<li>Be willing to overcome traditional boundaries of exchange, that is, reach outside your comfort zone to try something new or different.</li>
<li>Develop partnerships within the arts sector/community among artists, arts organizations, and cultural stakeholders.</li>
<li>Develop partnerships among arts ecosystem creators/presenters, intermediaries, and residents/government/business.</li>
</ul>
</td></tr>
</table>

<table>
<tr><td colspan="3">Cultural development: long-term, multi-dimensional, multi-beneficial, self-sustainable</td></tr>
<tr><td></td><td></td><td>

- Pursue holistic development that benefits individual organizations and sector-wide outcomes.
- Highlight your individual, community, and creative distinctiveness.
- Ensure reciprocal, viable benefits for all stakeholders and contributors.
- Incorporate social return on investment (SROI), quality of life, and social impacts (generally with a long view toward measurable impacts).
- Maintain support for events/festivals but consider how to expand initiatives, partnerships, and spin-offs (for artists) that generate ongoing income and are deep-rooted beyond service and gig-economies.
- Focus expansion efforts on year-round economic development.

</td></tr>
</table>

Social return on investment (SROI) is a method for measuring values that are not traditionally reflected in financial statements, including social, economic, and environmental impacts. SROI can identify how effectively a company uses its capital and other resources to create value for the community.

Consideration #2: Public awareness and Engagement
Public awareness of and engagement in arts, culture, and heritage
<ul><li>Utilize communication, training, and public relations methods that integrate residents, business, artists, municipal employees, and politicians with arts sector initiatives.</li><li>Invite any arts ecosystem stakeholders to participate in development opportunities and execution processes.</li></ul>
Emphasis toward the *value* of arts and culture
<ul><li>Advocate that neither artists nor their work should be perceived as *supplements* in either societal or vertical integration (business, government) contexts but are *core* to the structure and processes of long-term economic development.</li></ul>
Knowledge building and perception of artistic creative development
<ul><li>Provide local initiatives that shares knowledge with the purpose to invite engagement, specifically diminishing (self-imposed) barriers to inclusion through modelling.</li><li>Exploit local assets and resources to attract attention as a means for artistic, professional development.</li><li>Develop local (scalable) platforms that invite knowledge exchange between artists, between stakeholders, and among sectors.</li></ul>

Consideration #3: Embracing heritage in new ways

	Re-imagine local heritage
	<ul><li>Develop and discover new and engaging stories that expose your history.</li><li>Envision and present new options to include both traditional and new digital formats.</li><li>Move from current or traditional perceptions to include hidden, emerging, and present-day (contemporary) heritage.</li><li>Expand from *quaint or traditional* to _____ (that which aligns with a multi-pronged vision benefiting multiple stakeholders).</li></ul>

Contemporary and historical creative works co-existing as emerging assets
<ul><li>Move beyond established anchors of success; incorporate and develop new product (e.g. creative clusters, co-operatives/shops, artist studios, auditioned street entertainers – with quality control).</li><li>Integrate technology to explore or exploit historical contexts (e.g. interactive walking maps, subject-specific public art – like historical figures or events, light shows).</li><li>Promote architecture that is specific and unique to your locale.</li><li>Introduce themes and programming that build upon established knowledge or initiate new curiosities about local assets.</li></ul>

CHAPTER SUMMARY

- This chapter summarizes analysis from *The Focus Matrix*. The detailed matrix is available at www.proctorshiftconsulting.com at the *My Book* page.

- There are six primary artistic drivers that support the principal stakeholder of the arts ecosystem, the artist. This individual is identified as the principal stakeholder given that their artistic creativity ignites the larger arts ecosystem.

- Six primary artistic drivers are associated with an artists' presence:
    - Creative works
    - Place
    - Linkages to traditional and non-traditional arts ecosystem stakeholders
    - Non-financial resources (focussing on local resources and assets)
    - Visioning
    - Economics

- The artistic drivers intersect with other stakeholders within the arts ecosystem, providing a shared opportunity for mutual benefit.

- The seven arts ecosystem stakeholders are:
    - Artists (principal stakeholders of the ecosystem)
    - Arts organizations
    - Heritage and museum organizations and properties

- o   Residents
- o   Municipality
- o   Business
- o   Provincial/state government

6

Benefits That Artists Influence

This chapter identifies potential impacts for arts ecosystem *stakeholders* (artists, arts organizations, heritage & museum properties, residents, municipalities, business, provinces/states) within the ecosystem. Although not absolute, impacts outlined for one stakeholder can directly support, correlate to, align with, or replicate impacts of another stakeholder.

These intersections between ecosystem stakeholders create opportunities for mutually beneficial partnerships. They also provide arts administrators occasions to advocate and share their knowledge while bridging trust, understanding, and community building through partnerships.

On journeys of discovery, we often crave the end result right away. We want to jump into the *answer queue*, that is, reproduce what is already in place, rather than do the hard work toward finding an appropriate and innovative answer. I will spare you this urge to jump ahead by leading with a summary outline of the benefits and potential impacts that reflect each stakeholder group.

In the next two sections of this chapter, I begin with a focus on the artist. From the list of primary stakeholders, the artist is the critical driver. The artist is the stimulus for the ecosystem.

First, I introduce the **benefits** of having artists in your community. Second, I introduce benefits and tactics that *other primary stakeholders* can **leverage** from artists' presence. The intersections in the arts ecosystem reflect artists' creativity, their artwork and broader economic developments spurred by layers of spin-off effects due to the artist's presence.

This present chapter drills into how each stakeholder intersects with the **artist's** presence in their community. If you question why something is stated as a benefit, I provide further explanation in Chapter 7, *Intersecting Drivers and Stakeholders*. There I present each *artistic driver* (creative works, place, linkages to the art ecosystem, non-financial resources, visioning, economics) and cross-reference how each driver intersects with *all* stakeholders (artists, arts organizations, heritage & museum properties, residents, municipalities, business, province/state). The details presented in Chapter 7 ground the research findings not only outlined in this chapter but also included throughout this book.

You might find it helpful to keep a reference list of the ecosystem stakeholders and the artistic drivers as you read these next two chapters. This may help you digest and clarify what presents as overlapping information in some cases. They are listed in the previous paragraph and in Chapter 5 under the section entitled *Artists: Primary Drivers of the Arts Ecosystem* with sub-headings *Six Artistic Drivers* and *Seven Stakeholders*.

A seventh artistic driver, *education*, emerged (marginally) from my original research. As it was not a predominant element of the arts ecosystem, I did not include it in my summary list throughout the book. Education and creative advancement are critical for artistic excellence. Learning opportunities allow for evolution and adaptation of techniques, materials, or general growth in chosen disciplines. Education is offered through arts organizations, residencies, online courses, exchange programs, and other educational formats. The optimal learning platform might include hands-on, in-person, or online teaching methods, depending on the discipline and access to instructors. Artist-in-residence programs are highly valued by artists across many disciplines.

Let's begin.

The Artist as the Critical Driver/Principal Stakeholder

As the **critical driver**, the artist is also the principal stakeholder in the arts and cultural ecosystem. An artist exists within a livelihood that constructs value from meagre beginnings. Their work results from a creative spark, an idea, a need to create something that tells a story or translates their insight into desired arts forms. Their work may encompass physical, tangible works such as public art or a hand-crafted object; other forms might include intangible experiences such as listening to music or watching a live performance.

Artists create in unique spaces that address their creative needs—natural light, water, electricity, paint splashes, kilns— and strive to do so for minimal cost. Studios may comprise home-based areas, artist collectives, shared spaces, or otherwise unused space for minimal (if any) cost. Creative presentation spaces include 'pop-up' performances or visual art exhibitions among an array of public, vacant, mobile, traditional, and increasingly unique spaces.

Some artists repurpose discarded items reducing negative environmental impacts while fashioning materials into a new item of value. Many artists and their artwork support environmental stewardship.

Commissioned works generate reliable income for artists and often expose new audiences, as in the example of public art, award designs, portraits, and other offerings. Commissioned works are often highly valued as they assure payment for artistic creation.

Artworks influence the quality of life for residents and communities, especially when direct engagement co-exists among multiple stakeholders. Over time, artistic communities and their collective works reflect a community fabric and influence economic development, directly and indirectly. That which makes it unique (the vibe, art studios, retail shops) attracts locals, tourists, and other diverse populations.

Arts ecosystem stakeholders strategically leverage public response to artists' creative offerings to attract business expansion and relocation for educational, creative, and technological sectors, and entice conference activities or festivals. This broad appeal contributes to a layering effect that supports a community's overall diversity and sustainability.

Artists themselves are diverse in how they think, their scope of practice, and messages their artworks communicate. Traditionally, artists work in stable mediums, meaning they create work that will endure for many generations. An artist's purpose is often to reflect the world as they see it, which may mean challenging the status quo when bringing a new (or some may say outrageous) perspective on their chosen topic. Their insight can be visionary, often peeling back layers that reveal another aspect to an otherwise common story. Artists weave their insights into song, dance, visual art, theatre, digital platforms, books, video, and other art forms. Their work can both challenge and enlighten our ideas and understanding of a topic. Nuanced messages may be presented through fictional characters and environments. The options are infinite, as is the creativity of artists!

Artistic insight and output benefit ecosystem stakeholders, such as drawing tourists who then purchase accommodation. Absent direct interaction with artists or arts organizations, business owners may not consider artists' presence as an indirect benefit that supports their business interests. Impacts from artists' presence often ripple through communities and, over time, take root. There are exceptions.

The lists below highlight how **arts ecosystem stakeholders** (arts organizations and arts sector intermediaries, heritage and museum properties, residents, municipalities, business, provincial/state government) can benefit from artist's presence in their community. Consider leveraging these benefits when reflecting on 'place' and how artists' work connects to broader, long-term economic considerations for stakeholders *and* the artist.

Arts Organizations and Arts Sector Intermediaries

Arts organizations work in direct contact with artists. They are often the link between core artistic creators and the promotion and/or presentation of an artist's work. This group includes service organizations (arts councils, professional accreditation services, and similar entities), theatres, shared studio spaces, galleries, dance studios, and other resources that support the artist and may offer public-facing or membership-only programming.

- **Infrastructure**: Establishing venues (traditional and untraditional) to present creative works directly support artists' creative output, offering necessary presentation elements such as technical, rehearsal, public facing, and retail opportunities. More and more 'pop up' activities occur anywhere and anytime, offering the option of a temporary venue.

- **Arts sector anchor**: Arts organizations are a significant contributor to a vibrant cultural community, often (but not always) within a municipality's cultural district. Cultural hubs and creative hubs are becoming common one-stop gathering locations for artists, audiences, arts organizations, and community groups.

- **Networking**: The very nature of an arts organization brings together multiple stakeholders who support an organization's mandate. Often the organization is the hub of artist-driven networks. Take advantage of your various networks by sharing information, inviting participation, or offering partnership ideas that connect and benefit members of multiple networks locally, nationally, internationally.

- **Cross-marketing**: Leaders of arts organization can influence the marketing content of other stakeholders. When investigating partnership collaborations, consider how to best position the external stakeholder in both their and your promotional materials. The message to each audience is probably different; ensure messaging, target audiences and platforms align for each stakeholder's benefit.

- **Education and training**: Many arts organizations or their members offer training, workshops, or community classes. These programs increase local engagement, break down barriers to inclusion, attract new (potential) patrons to the arts, and support learning for personal and professional levels of knowledge and well-being.

- **Attracting new residents/inclusion**: 'Next generation' cultural sector development focuses on community development. Incorporate arts activities to inspire inclusion, social engagement, and building neighbourhoods. Offer initiatives to all local residents, but especially newcomer, immigrant, racialized, Indigenous and equity-seeking populations.

Heritage and Museums

Heritage properties and museums increasingly work to attract more visitors. They actively seek partnerships to host community events and offer unique programming within their facilities that might be promoted through tourism initiatives. Leaders strategically position and expand their operations to incorporate new prospects that may include artistic contributions.

- **Branding**: Historical assets describe and identify the culture of its residents, building stories and the fabric of a place that further support branding for municipal and tourism initiatives.

- **Tourism draw**: A distinct—and growing—segment of tourists travel to discover histories and visit historical sites to explore the stories and architecture of a place.

- **Programming**: An emerging trend involves historical locations and museums hosting arts and cultural programming activities to increase foot traffic and revenues as part of strategic sustainable planning initiatives. Primary programming in these institutions tells your community's story!

Residents

Anyone who lives in a community or district populated by artists is considered a resident affected (directly or indirectly) by the artists' presence in their area.

- **Healthy society**: Many studies recognize how study or enjoyment of the arts contributes toward long-term health benefits. Active or passive arts participation supports physical, mental, and social inclusion; acceptance; and community building. This point is made repeatedly in this book; its importance deserves restatement within multiple contexts.

- **Vitality**: An active arts community brings enjoyment, new experiences, and education through expression of world events, historical topics, societal issues, celebrations, and other themes. The arts expose the diversity-of-thought in a community that stimulates new and traditional applications.

- **Communal and social engagement**: Artistic works activate creative opportunities for public engagement through their presentation within social gathering spaces. Cross-pollination among those external with those internal to the arts sector—by working outside of traditional comfort zones—encourages acceptance, empathy, and broader views. This, in turn, influences creative and independent thinking. Engagement in artistic disciplines is particularly important for children and youth to develop these important skills to carry throughout their lives. Activating community and social initiatives create pathways that can contribute to a 'healthy society'.

- **Diversity**: A community that actively embraces arts and culture attracts the attention of businesses and those people who look to relocate and establish new (local) business development opportunities. These activities add diversity to both the local economy and the population, melding and enriching the lives of all residents.

Municipality

Municipalities are political districts with a governing body of staff and politically-appointed decision makers. A municipality plays an important role in developing the local arts ecosystem, noticeably through policies that do (or do not) support arts sector intermediaries and the artists they represent.

It is important for arts sector champions within municipal structures to encourage their municipality's *consistent* support for arts sector development through integrated sustainability. Inconsistent levels of support challenge an arts administrator's ability to accurately plan over the long term, lessening their ability to leverage third party support, increasing the potential for unstable programming, staffing, and economic returns. When artists and arts intermediaries succeed, the ripple effect in local economies—and social integration, cohesion, and health of citizens—reaches across municipalities through broad impacts and benefits for an increased number of residents. Understandably, this list is remarkably similar to *Residents* (above).

- **Attractiveness of a place**: Promotes the essence of a community through social activities, tourism strategies, business activities, modern conveniences, historical architecture, and collections. The public presence of artists and their creative outputs influence a community's vibe, atmosphere, and general attractiveness, such as, what is illustrated through public art (murals, sculptures, street art, performances).

- **Quality of life**: Municipalities want to offer a high quality of life for residents. Businesses seeking expanded markets carefully consider and are attracted by a community's high quality of life index. The same can be said for newcomers who often seek to establish a new life for their family in a place that offers a wide range of creative attractions and opportunities.

- **Competitive advantage**: Unique, original, and not-easily-replicated community assets exemplify its distinctiveness. Artistic matter adds to that distinctiveness. Municipalities can magnify these assets in their promotional efforts, especially when exposing either singular elements or a combination of assets that express value or uniqueness beyond the obvious!

- **Communal and social engagement**: Artistic works can entice public engagement, most often when presented in social gathering spaces. This presentation encourages cross-pollination of arts sector stakeholders while influencing qualities like acceptance, empathy, and broad views that inspire creative and independent thinking.

- **Healthy society**: Studies recognize how study and enjoyment of the arts contributes to long-term health benefits whether through acting, singing, playing musical instruments, writing, painting, watching, or listening to another's performance. Both active and passive participation in the arts support physical and mental well-being, social inclusion; acceptance; and community building. A healthy society directly affects not only residents, but also municipal planning and spending considerations in developing desired outcomes.

- **Activates the creative pillar of cultural vitality**: Sustainable communities are built upon four pillars: Economic Prosperity, Environmental Sustainability, Social Equity, and Cultural Vitality. The fourth pillar of *cultural vitality* links prominently to *economic prosperity*, and *social equity* through economic ripple effects and social well-being outcomes.[xxiv]

Business

The business sector is a vital cog in the economic wheel. Many businesses generously contribute to their community through philanthropic initiatives and donations to not-for-profit organizations. Donations may include in-kind donations of product or services, many forms of sponsorship support, direct financial support, access to promotional platforms, or additional types of resources. Local business working in the service and tourism sectors (such as restaurants and hotels) are often the first to realize their business benefits from arts and cultural sector activities. When festivals, cultural districts, theatres, music, street art, and other art forms attract visitors, service-industry businesses are well-positioned to capture incoming market revenues.

Those businesses that gain *indirect* impacts from arts and cultural activities may not realize the importance of trickle-down impacts on their business, such as employee satisfaction, a creative workforce, and their staffs' solution-oriented approach to problem solving. These impacts, however, relate directly to artists' presence in your community. Further, businesses often realize direct benefit when supporting local community initiatives, but many have not been approached to engage in partnerships.

- **Staff engagement**: A business can develop corporate social responsibility (CSR) programs encouraging their staffs' participation in broader societal and cultural activities. The business benefits through increased public awareness of their company's support for local arts initiatives and staff are energized by personal involvement, which may translate into greater enthusiasm and better focus at work.

- **Community support**: A business that builds partnerships with arts and community organizations is investing in their community and are well-positioned to receive reciprocal business and community support. Direct benefits may include new customers, increased media coverage, and ripple effects generated by positive word of mouth in the community.

- **Immigration retention**: By supporting not-for-profit organizations, a company expands its reach to potential clients new to their community. Outreach to new immigrants has been linked to immigrant retention and community integration, giving a sense of welcome—an important aspect of community building—a feeling of inclusion, and developing business/client relationships.

Provincial/State Government

Similar to municipalities, provincial/state or regional governments are a governing body of staff and politically-appointed members. The province/state or region plays an important role in developing their arts ecosystem, noticeably through policy and other measures of support for both artists and arts sector intermediaries.

Arts champions within provincial/state or regional government structures are encouraged to educate their colleagues toward *consistent* support for arts sector development and sustainability. Consistently aligned policies, combined with financial support, reduce year-to-year uncertainty and provide arts administrators confidence when developing budgets and programming schedules. In any sector, stable business environments increase the potential for organizations to meet strategic outcomes while generating audiences and deepening their intrinsic value in the community over the long term.

- **Business / Resident relocation**: Creative cities and creative communities are an important pillar for government in their efforts to attract residents, business, tourism, and student interest. Using this knowledge to promote creative *value* through marketing materials holds substantial weight that, over the long-term, encourages diverse populations to seek, visit, and live in these places.

- **Quality of life**: Creative artworks and cultural offerings support community learning, diversity, and engagement in other cultures – particularly for people external to exhibited traditions. Offering a high quality of life to residents is important for governments but also to businesses seeking market and workforce expansion. Communities that offer diversity and wide-ranging social inclusion activities rank highly with residents, business, and government leaders.

- **Immigration**: Social integration and inclusion through the arts is a gateway for melding diversity into neighbourhood building. Community activation and diversity modelling through the arts is especially effective for newcomers who have limited knowledge of yet desire to belong in their new home/neighbourhood. Welcoming newcomers through inclusion in the arts promotes immigrant retention and overall community integration.

- The artist is a **critical driver** and the principal stakeholder in the arts and cultural ecosystem.

- Some artists repurpose used or discarded items (sometimes for little or no cost). This both reduces negative environmental impacts and infuses value into newly-fashioned, yet previously rejected, materials.

- Artworks influence quality of life metrics for residents and communities, especially when direct engagement exists among multiple stakeholders.

- An artist's purpose is often to reflect the world as they see it, which may mean challenging the status quo when bringing new perspectives to bear. Their insights can be visionary, often peeling back layers that reveal other aspects of a common story.

- Artistic insight and output benefits other primary stakeholders in the ecosystem. In the absence of working directly with arts sector stakeholders, indirect benefits can often go unnoticed. Trickle-down beneficiaries may, unknowingly, devalue or ignore the link between what artists organically construct and how their presence influences beneficiaries' business revenues.

- Arts sector champions positively influence *consistent* support for the arts sector. Inconsistent levels of municipal backing challenge an arts administrator's ability to leverage third party support, influencing long-term programming, staffing, and economic returns.

- Businesses that gain *indirectly* from arts and cultural activities may be oblivious to intrinsic benefits on their business, such as employee satisfaction, a creative workforce, and their staffs' solution-oriented approach to problem solving.

Case Study: "Open House" in York, Alabama. Artist: Matthew Mazzotta

RE: INVITING INPUT AND INCLUSION = COMMUNITY PRIDE AND OWNERSHIP

Open House is a community-based, artist-in-residence-led project that highlights how social and community engagement transforms a street: a community.

Matthew Mazzotta, artist-in-residence at Coleman Centre for the Arts in York, Alabama, invited community members (literally) into the street with furniture from their homes to facilitate discussion around a new public art project. Community members decided to transform a 'blighted property' in their downtown into a unique, public event space. Materials from the abandoned residence were used to construct a new smaller 'house' on the original property.

The resulting structure transforms into a 100-seat open-air theatre free for the public to use as a gathering place to support their community life. The reconfigured public space invites presentations of movies, plays, music, and other special events. When not in use, the rows of seats fold up into the shape of a 'house.' Seeing repurposed materials in the reconfigured 'house' is a reminder of the past while celebrating the property's transformation into a new public park.

This project brings the community together in the ideation of the project and through hands-on involvement in the building and enjoyment of the property. The ongoing impact of inclusion, social integration, and community spirit encourages caring and engaged citizens who take pride of their accomplishment and have ownership of their neighborhood.

This project was facilitated through the Coleman Artist-in-Residence program, along with partnerships among municipal, business, arts, and, community members. The project occurred between 2011 and 2013, commencing with communal idea generation and culminating in community members using the revitalized outdoor space.

The Coleman Centre in York, Alabama fosters art for positive social change.

Part 2

Applying Research and Developing Strategies

7

Intersecting Drivers and Stakeholders

During my EMBA studies, I was introduced to academic and peer-reviewed articles (meaning critically reviewed by other academics before being published) for the first time. A world of research opened up to me. I eagerly dove into 'rabbit holes' exploring various topics. I found data that addressed cross-cutting impacts among multiple stakeholders within the arts ecosystem. When I compiled my findings, many benefactors, intermediaries, and drivers had web-like interconnections, yet each stakeholder propelled its individual purpose and focus within the ecosystem. The mass of information intertwined, overlapped, and took time to tease out.

My analysis revealed a unique perspective from which each stakeholder could influence the larger arts ecosystem. I confirmed that outputs generated from a vibrant arts sector benefit multiple stakeholders, generating and influencing stakeholder-specific outcomes across the spectrum. I saw strong linkages among artworks, artists, and arts organizations as drivers of social and financial outcomes that extend into local communities.

For example, from an economic development perspective one might expect that festivals or tourism drive attraction to a municipality, and they do. But where does the content for that festival or tourist attraction come from? Often, content that attracts attention is creative output of an artist or group of artists. Therefore, when we reframe this economic development initiative to reflect the artist as the driver based on their delivery of artistic content, the festival and all that it entails becomes an intermediary. The municipality, its residents, and tourism industry stakeholders become the beneficiaries.

If the artist drives the content, is the artist also a beneficiary? That depends on the context and on how the work is distributed.

Who in the arts ecosystem leads and who follows? Again, that depends. At what point of the arts ecosystem value chain and/or supply chain does the transaction for creative artwork take place?

My research demonstrated that artistic content created by the driver of the arts ecosystem (the artist) has a ripple effect across economic and social systems. Other ecosystem stakeholders contribute also; when we consider the entire arts ecosystem, we see how each part fits into the whole. We can then acknowledge the contribution of how each benefits the other and, ultimately, the entire webbed membership.

As ideal as that sounds, we are not 'there' yet; fractures in the holistic model remain.

For example, what is the distance (time, money, number of intermediaries) between an artistic creation and the economic return to the artist? How or through whom is the artist paid if not directly by a transactional exchange or sale? Do stakeholders or benefactors at arms-length from the artist consider it appropriate to compensate for intangible artistic property layered into their own work, such as ideas generated through consultation with an artist? Or perhaps benefactors choose to reinvest in the artist's creative process, so ongoing benefits from their work continue to flow throughout the ecosystem? If so, how is this triggered?

These are daunting questions that all arts ecosystem stakeholders need to consider. Reflecting on these questions should elevate respect for artistic works and bring broader awareness of not only their value that underscores the ecosystem, but also the need for increased compensation attributed to that value. Above all else, artists need the time, space and compensation level that allows them to focus on their core area of expertise – artistic creation.

When applying this same thought process to the local level, what makes it possible for an artist to live and survive in your community? How and why did they choose to come? What brought them there? What makes them stay?

Investigating these questions, I identified six recurring core elements that support an artistic practice and influence where an artist will live. These artistic drivers are creative works, place, linkages to the arts ecosystem, non-financial resources, visioning, and economics. Each of these drivers were introduced in Chapter 5 and are explored in this chapter.

Community stakeholders are well positioned to support artists' works. Understanding what community assets attract artists and learning how to connect to them opens the door for cultivation of mutually beneficial relationships that, ultimately, support artists.[xxv] Recognize artists as humans with a predisposition for giving to others. It is equally important for stakeholders not to take advantage of artists' generosity but rather to value it deeply.

How This Information Informs You

Here is where we peel back the next layer. This is where the gold is!

How do **artistic drivers** influence relationship building between an artist, arts organization, and other arts ecosystem stakeholders? To answer this question, first, I outline each of the six artistic drivers. Then, I analyze each artistic driver to show how it interconnects with the corresponding primary stakeholder: arts organizations, heritage and museums, residents, municipalities, business, and government.

In each case, I cross-reference potential opportunity for individual arts ecosystem stakeholders. I also highlight multiple points of intersection *between* ecosystem stakeholders. This detailed information corresponds to the summary of benefits for each stakeholder, as noted in the previous chapter.

Artistic Driver #1: Creative Works

Creative works are an artist's creative output, regardless of their chosen discipline. The conditions that support artistic output are varied and include where an artist lives, their access to resources, infrastructure, audiences, and many other factors.

Many artists prefer to reside in an area where their work can find local public display or presentation, therefore translating into social engagement and interaction opportunities in public and indoor venues. Often, an artist has a positive impact on their physical environment through reuse of discarded or second-use materials, which requires access to such materials and has the added benefit of reducing garbage waste. Many aspects of creative development or production are accomplished with a keen eye to a low environmental impact. Working in this way also reduces overall expenses and the financial outlay required to create art.

Artistic purpose generates contemplation but also encourages discussion. Artwork can relate stories of historical events or imaginative fantasy, often drawing attention through social or intellectual engagement in their work.

Some works are politically motivated; therefore, artists need to live where they will be neither victimised for their work nor for the message it bears.

Regardless of the style or discipline of work, artistic *creators* generate IP and copyright of their artwork. These property rights must be respected. When copyright is not respected, artists do not receive payment for their IP and the resulting artwork. This inaction is taking property without payment to the rightful owner. For example, using an image or a song in a marketing campaign or a playwright's script for scholastic purposes requires payment to the rightful owner. When any form of art or IP is copied, reused, or distributed, payment is due to the artist, the creator. The impact of not paying for IP supresses an artist's livelihood, devalues their time and effort, and adds financial pressure, leaving them to seek alternative revenue sources to survive – abandoning their artistic practice either partially or entirely to do so. The imbalance leaves artists struggling to survive within the very ecosystem they incubate, yet their viability is vital to envision and produce artistic matter from which all other stakeholders' benefit.

It is in everyone's social, economic, and creative benefit to champion artistic value and appropriate payment for artists' work.

Linking to Other Arts Ecosystem Stakeholders

So how does the artistic driver **creative works** intersect stakeholders within the local arts ecosystem? In this section, I summarize potential outputs and opportunities linked to creative artistic works. Each ecosystem stakeholder is highlighted, followed by a list of potential associated benefits. This format continues until all stakeholders are noted.

Conditions and opportunities often overlap among multiple stakeholders simultaneously. Suggested considerations and tactics may apply to more than one stakeholder, potentially resulting in similar or different outcomes for each stakeholder. Shared benefits suggest multi-stakeholder partnerships hold increased value among associated partners, offering mutually-beneficial opportunity.

The lists provided are not all-inclusive. Dovetail your approach to partnerships based on the conditions, assets, and resources in your community. I encourage you to generate ideas that reflect your own organization and your own community.

Arts Organizations

Programming: Creative works are displayed, presented, or supported through development phases to further enhance or distribute them. Create partnerships between artists, community groups, municipal offices, and businesses to weave artistic programming into office space, festivals, celebrations, newcomer activities, healthcare facilities, and other forums. The arts organization is a prime facilitator for programming of this nature, given their close association with artists.

Education: Venues assemble exhibitions, talks, workshops, school field trips, and other activities that broaden understanding of the work and the stories behind artistic works. Develop programming that links to curriculum, local traditions, historical anniversaries, new and emerging initiatives, community groups, and other opportunities. Be mindful to invite local stakeholders across your doorstep, especially those not otherwise connected to the arts.

Public Art: Arts organizations often lead or support public art projects. They often collaborate with municipal, business, and artistic stakeholders. Public art consultants develop long-term plans focused on public art development. Work with them in association with other stakeholders to facilitate artists' input into the process.

Advocacy: Arts organizations are a leading voice that advocates on behalf of artists. They intimately understand the purpose and value of these core artistic creators. Advocacy work dovetails into building a supportive infrastructure for the sector, discipline-based training, public presentations, audience development, and skillfully built relationships. Shifting your focus to educate the public develops opportunities to engage and expand local (or larger) cross-sectoral industries.

Heritage and Museums

Heritage properties and museums are increasingly being used to support artistic works through their programming, which attracts more visitors to these sites. They actively seek partnerships to host community and unique programming within their facilities that may be promoted through tourism and other publicity initiatives. Strategically positioning themselves and their operations to take advantage of new opportunities is prudent.

Programming: Creative works can be curated to reflect stories. Creative works can also complement programming through focused cycles during the organization's calendar year, potentially off-site. (Also see the last item in this list: *Hub Space.*)

Collections and Research: Heritage vaults and museums gather, disseminate, and act as the keeper of traditions, while seeking deep knowledge of topical areas. Work with these stakeholders to both give to and draw from traditions and collections, including local stories, artwork, music, and other creative works.

Education: These venues assemble exhibitions, talks, workshops, school field trips, and other activities to broaden our understanding of the work and the stories behind displays and artwork. Historical contexts might be presented by actors in period costume who lead tours down city streets or re-enact activities in historical villages.

Hub Space: Strategically speaking, hub spaces are developing as focal points for multiple types of community and artistic gatherings—individual studio workspace, workshops, presentations, and other venues—to present creative works. Increased use of a facility can be a measure of an institution's sustainability. An example is a church repurposed into a community space for meetings, art classes, performances, and so on.

Residents

Anyone living in a specific community or district are residents of that area and are affected by local artistic presence directly and indirectly, knowingly and unknowingly.

Entertainment: Residents passively and actively enjoy different forms of artwork including public (no admission) presentations in-person or through digital online platforms. Transactional purchases garner tangible and intangible experiences. Art pieces may be seen, heard, explored, or owned.

Education: Residents gain knowledge through the stories depicted in the artwork. As knowledge deepens, it fosters broad-minded thinking and may generate additional interest in the specific discipline, artist, or the topic. Public workshops are excellent opportunities that welcome the general public to discover an artistic practice or an artist.

Social integration / Community building: Artwork creates gathering space for residents to both interact and engage with artwork and each other. Consider including an artistic discipline as a gateway to social engagement and integration of attendees, regardless of the context, such as public concerts, collaborative murals, or interactive public art.

Intellectually: Traditional (sometimes called analog) creative works such as dance, visual art, many forms of music, and other customs of artistic practice influence our perceptions of time, space, and possibility. These stable media are based on human ideation and construction. They allow for observation, deliberation, contemplation, and scrutiny of ourselves and societies.

> *Author's Note*: Digital creative works are formed through unstable media as noted in Chapter 3.

Municipality

Municipalities are governed by staff and politically-appointed decision makers, and thus play an important role in developing the local arts ecosystem. It is very important for champions of the arts within municipal structures to encourage consistent support for arts sector development, leading to long-term sustainability of the local sector.

Policy: Ensure policy and planning initiatives support access to and distribution of artists' creative matter, as impacted by signage bylaws, loading zones, festival permits, public art, and other regulations. Facilitate artists' inclusion in development of sector-specific legislation to address specific concerns, barriers, vision, and opportunities first-hand to policy makers. Without arts sector input areas of concern may, otherwise, be shielded from view of councillors and city staff.

Financial: Establish a funding envelope (such as grants and bursaries) that invests directly in creative time, space, artwork, and programming for artists and arts organizations. Consider what next-phase support looks like in your community, moving artworks into expanded creative development (such as dramaturge, music recording, or mass production or printing), ideally at a local level. Consider how the artwork can benefit from exhibition or distribution outside the local area (that is, consider touring or digital platform distribution networks) besides those who are ideal partners locally, regionally or at state level, nationally, and internationally.

Niche marketing: Use locally-produced artistic works that support your corporation's marketing efforts, such as for attracting new or relocating businesses, tourism initiatives, or overall branding purposes. Pay the artist a commission when using their image, artwork, music, voice, or when referring to their work. Establish partnerships with arts organizations, artists, galleries, and other arts sector intermediaries to promote local artistic works while establishing revenue opportunities for artists, firmly rooting the opportunities within local economic impacts.

Power distance: Reduce the power distance relationship between the city/town hall and artists. Build relationships that invite artists' participation through their expertise, knowledge, and their networks. Given the previously-noted polar opposite objectives of business and art, consider working through an arts organization to establish an initial connection; build your relationships and trust from there.

Municipal consumption: Buy artworks outright for public display, annual presentation, or gifts; commission awards or conference lanyards; value local artists and their work. Promote artists and their unique works in your marketing materials, paying them standard rates to appear in promotional materials. Invite artists to present or give a talk about their artistic practice at meetings, receptions, openings, special events, and unique venues.

Hybrid employment: Consider short-term or casual employment contracts that bring artists' creative expertise and visioning skills to municipal projects. Many artists work within the gig economy and hold both broad and unique skillsets outside of their artistic practice. Consider working through an intermediary (such as an arts council) to find an appropriate match of skills within desired disciplines to deliver required output.

Business

Many businesses appreciate the impact creative artwork has in their community and they respond through philanthropic initiatives that support non-profit organizations. Donations may be in-kind product or services, sponsorship support, financial resources, promotional platforms, or involve several valued resources. The window of opportunity between arts organizations and businesses in this area of the arts ecosystem is wide. Finding the right partner, crafting unique benefits, and promoting the partnership can pay significant dividends generated through publicity, curiosity, engagement, social, and 'feel good' factors that help fulfill corporate social responsibility goals.

Partnerships: Businesses often support events or initiatives through financial or in-kind resources; consider shared physical and digital platforms and digital presentations. Three-way partnerships leverage broader support and expand the reach for an initiative. By involving the staff of an external partner, you help to reduce reluctance toward arts participation while influencing teamwork and enhancing leadership skills within their organization.

Community engagement: Support development and presentation of local creative works. Corporate social responsibility programs develop creative engagement that weaves philanthropy with community support through financial, volunteering, matching programs (financial donations), art studio space allocation, and many other means. A business that taps into local community needs often develops the most successful corporate social responsibility programs.[xxvi] The public is eager to support businesses that support their community. Reciprocal partnerships deepen the rootedness of each stakeholder driving a stronger local economy. Each organization can realize operational and competitive advantages, especially when aligning their resources to address community need and contribute to positive outcomes.

Market consumption: Buy local artwork, music, juried artisan products, and other creative works as gifts for clients; buy directly from artists, or artist co-operatives. Adorn offices with locally made sculpture, visual art, and contemporary art pieces acquired through a public gallery, cooperative, or directly from an artist. Consider presentation modes that passively sell artworks while championing local artists, series of their works, and their local value. Include artists who are clients in your marketing materials and tell a story that profiles both their work and your support for their artistic contribution to your community.

Hybrid employees: Hire artists for conference murals or presentations; contract them for creative brainstorming/designing/planning sessions within areas of mutual interest and knowledge. If you don't have direct contact with artists, consider working with an arts (council) administrator to navigate how to find an artist whose expertise aligns with the company's values/needs.

Government

Elected officials and their staff at a provincial or regional/state levels of government play an important role in developing the arts sector ecosystem. As with municipal officials, provincial, and regional/state government champions should encourage consistent support for arts sector development and sustainability.

Policy: Ensure policies, legislation, and planning initiatives support access to and distribution of artists' creative output, such as strategic initiatives, laws and bylaws, touring/festival permits, artist exchange residencies, and building occupancy/business usage. Ensure that artists are not only consulted but also have a permanent voice at the table in all levels of government to ensure their concerns, barriers, vision, and opportunities are presented first-hand to policy makers.

Cultural Diplomacy: Artwork creates space to both interact and engage with others. Consider adding artistic disciplines within agendas and programs as a gateway to social integration of attendees—particularly when hosting international delegates—at formal meetings or discussions among provinces, states, or countries. Suggested content might include musical presentations, collaborative works, or interactive art pieces.

Marketing: Celebrating the presence of artists, arts organizations, and their creative work will increase the likelihood they are valued and considered authentic resources in your community. A broad focus might include showcasing support of the arts sector, the vibrancy of a local society, or the value the arts sector brings to economic development through festivals, activities, unique products, and events.

Tourism: Tourists want to experience local traditions, activities, tangible products, and events—ideally with locals. A vibrant arts and cultural sector is a strong attractant, directly or as an add-on to conventions, meetings, or other activities. Consider contacting arts sector leaders to build initiatives that leverage artists' expertise, increase the perception of and tangible value for artistic matter, and enhance a visitor's experience.

Power distance and planning: Reduce the power distance relationship between all levels of government representatives (namely federal, provincial, state, and municipal levels) and artists, particularly when the arts sector is affected by government planning initiatives. Ideally, collaborate with an intermediary such as an arts service organization or arts council. Invite local artists and arts leader to convene and build trust and inter-reliance among stakeholders.

Provincial / State consumption: Provincial and state governments can buy artworks outright for public display in their offices, annual presentations, or gifts; commission specific pieces; promote artists and their work in marketing materials; invite local artists to inform government audiences of their artwork by invitation to meetings and/or receptions.

Hybrid employment: Artists are familiar with working in a gig economy. Consider short-term or casual employment contracts that take advantage of artists' creative and visioning skills. Work with an intermediary (such as an arts service organization) to ensure an appropriate match between artists and other partners. This model can lead to developing elasticity within a local workforce; that is, a workforce that expands, pivots, and contracts as economic sectors and seasonal demands warrant. A community that offers a flexible workforce is often desirable to businesses looking to relocate because of the diverse skillsets and culture of adaptability offered by potential employees.

Artistic Driver #2: Place

Like all people, artists require a place to live. However, artists often seek a location that inspires their creativity and perhaps offers a muse. The stimulation they seek can be associated with environmental beauty (rural or small urban areas or coastal areas) and specific resources that influence or support their work (may include urban areas). Rural and small urban areas offer a more affordable cost of living compared to larger urban centers, often with fewer barriers to establish themselves personally and professionally.

Large urban settings offer additional income opportunity for artists, such as teaching opportunities, gig-economy contract work that supports creative, tourism, health or other industries, and options to work in non-artistic professions that may (or may not) correlate with their creative aptitudes. Some employment is entered into as a matter of survival as opposed to the level of creative skill required or personal interest.

Overall, larger urban communities often offer greater diversity and career development opportunities for artists. Such offerings are partially due to larger, more established artistic communities and increased access to facilities and service organizations that support artists' work, including arts administrators. Citizens of larger urban centers tend to be more broad-minded and these environments tend to have more diverse cultures of origin because of higher levels of immigration and retention than rural or small urban communities.

Regardless of geographic location, artists often seek community-based, grounded linkages to their work, that is, their work reflects aspects of the community in which they live. Artists also consider locations that offer knowledge-based opportunities for themselves, such as artist-in-residence programs or skill development/advancement workshops. Artists communicate through their chosen discipline, often reflecting present-day society or visionary ideals, and act as a conduit to bring insights and messages to the world. In addition to affordability factors, many artists prefer to live where their work is appreciated and has opportunity to be valued, shared, discussed, and (ideally) purchased.

Where does the artistic driver **place** intersect with the arts ecosystem's stakeholders at the local level? The section that follows discusses how **primary stakeholders** (artists, arts organizations, heritage and museum properties, residents, municipalities, business, provinces, or states) can benefit from the presence of artists in their community. You will notice that conditions and opportunities often concurrently overlap among multiple stakeholders. The shared benefits that emerge suggest multi-stakeholder partnerships hold significant value among associated partners and are linked to value creation when seeking new opportunities.

The lists provided are suggestive, however, not all-inclusive. The prospects noted may influence how you think about developing new partnerships and should include local conditions, assets, and resources in your community. Generate your own ideas to best reflect your practice, your organization, and your community.

Arts organizations are recognizing they need to share resources and work together. As budgets and resources remain consistently lean, keeping pace with evolutionary and disruptive inputs requires embracing new ways of working together to not to just 'share the pie' but to actually 'build a bigger pie.' This air of collaboration is fertile ground to sprout and grow healthy partnerships. Asset-based and resource-based partnerships occur among arts organizations and between arts organizations and other arts ecosystem stakeholders.

Those stakeholders who are non-arts-centric can leverage many advantages when working with arts organizations; other opportunities not listed here may also exist in your community. Don't dismiss these opportunities; they may be equally or more valuable for your organization/business and your community.

Primary conduit to/from artists: Whether a presenting organization (theatre, gallery, or other venue), a service organization (arts council, professional arts administrators, foundation), or a studio (creative/retail), these spaces facilitate intersection between artists, managers, arts administrators, and the general public. Relationships with arts administrators can be a key access point to arts community membership.

Gathering place: Many arts organizations are brick and mortar spaces that double as meeting, performance, and creative spaces that gather a community of artists, other arts organizations, the general public or any combination of these and other activities. Consider the accumulated wisdom and skills these locations offer such as creative, technical, and other attributes and opportunities to engage multiple communities of people in one space.

Cultural hubs: Multi-purpose spaces house a variety of practitioners with retail and/or creative intention. This knowledge and talent are spread over larger geographic areas (called an arts or creative cluster). Within one building, a hub may present artists, arts administrators, and associated artwork and programming to the public – those who are curious to share, learn, collaborate, and/or purchase.

Collaboration / Capacity: Arts sector leaders are well-positioned to develop mutually beneficial relationships with municipal, business, and community leaders. They have direct access to artists and their artistic content (tangible and intangible). Arts administrators provide access for those who are curious about the arts; they can facilitate connections between the curious and the world of art. Accumulated interactive experiences reduce hesitancy in attending art venues or events should a person have little knowledge of the sector or art generally. This form of outreach builds both your network and knowledge within or outside the arts community and may pique new interest and enhanced levels of creative support.

Quality of life / Municipal branding: Artists' creative output translates into a vibrant community. Their work adorns promotional materials, expressed as assets to depict the quality of life for local branding initiatives. Arts organizations working with municipal and community partners can position artistic content as a strategic measure to benefit multiple stakeholders. You need to ensure a seat at the table to activate this opportunity.

> *Author's Note*: Arts administrators should be prepared
> to encounter perceptions that artists are 'erratic, overly
> emotional, crazy, or unrealistic' in your partnership
> approach. Use this opportunity to build a bridge of
> appreciation for artists, establish trust, and mitigate
> (perceived) risk, especially when working with non-arts-
> centric community leaders and their staff (see *Art In The
> Open* Case Study following Artistic Driver #2).

Heritage and Museums

The heritage and museums sector is a stakeholder that protects important stories of place. As a link between past and present-day realities, traditions, and intrinsic community layers, heritage and museums play an important role in the arts ecosystem.

Cultural identifiers: Heritage assets and museums provide traceable identifiers and stories of people and their traditions from a geographical area.

Infrastructure: Physical structure in a place takes on various forms depending on links to current or former industries (such as mining, agriculture, shipbuilding, or the fur trade), environmental feats (such as Ontario's Rideau Canal, a UNESCO World Heritage Site), local traditions, early immigrant settlements, or several geographic, economic, Indigenous, or social references.

Literature: Consider publications, books, magazines, and the desired preservation of these assets as important heritage identifiers. The evolution of tools used in development and dissemination of literature are also of heritage value as pertaining to newspapers, microfilm, pen quills, liquid ink bottles, and more.

Film and other media: Various media platforms are not always available; however, these offer another medium for exhibitions within a heritage and museum context. Within the evolution of communication and technology, museums capture abundant historical reference to early stage telephones, cameras, computers and much more.

Residents

Similar in importance to heritage and museums stakeholders, residents of a place embody stories, traditions, and ways of life that come together to create a mosaic within any community. People make the place!

Core values: A community's essence is reflected through core values adopted and exhibited by its residents. Artists, too, are residents.

Branding: Ownership of outcomes occurs when community membership has opportunity for input. Residents reflect authentic and distinctive community assets that can purposefully enhance branding initiatives when used strategically. Residents present broad points of view that can ignite unique opportunities, messaging, and collaborations.

Engagement: Residents are a primary target audience to build awareness, invite, and otherwise engage in artistic works. Forms of engagement may include ticketed, by donation, or no fee events, direct or indirect marketing, publicity strategies, volunteer opportunities, or accessibility that enables increased mobility or technological means.

Author's Note: Engagement is key to your public relations activities and will be discussed in Chapter 8, *Your Unique Assets.*

Value: How residents value artwork or artists is often connected to the importance of *short-term*, economic returns through product sales, tourism revenues, or festivals; this limited view does not consider social or other benefits. Rootedness in local communities strengthens an artist's value as does their influence through resident's participation, purchase, and word-of-mouth promotion of the creative work. Achieving long-term, societal, intellectual, health, creative, *and* economic benefits is tied to residents' holistic engagement, investment in and visioning of their community with artists.

Significant literature on the value of arts and culture has been published over many decades. For example, revenue-based statistics are compiled by Statistics Canada and are readily available through publications by Hill Strategies.[xxvii] Researchers are discovering new ways to measure the value and benefits of social and community well-being such as through the online, interactive, *Arts + Social Impact Explorer*.[xxviii] Published by Americans for the Arts, this tool links the value of the arts to participation in arts activities over and above economic impacts. For another example of how the arts influences more than just economic impacts, see the 2016 academic report by The Arts and Humanities Research Council in the United Kingdom entitled *Understanding the Value of Arts and Culture–The AHRC Cultural Value Project*, which addresses psychological, societal, economic, and other considerations.[xxix]

Municipality

Rural communities that seek to value the arts sector beyond economic generation are well positioned to benefit from social well-being and the inclusionary principles adopted from the second wave of arts sector development. Next generation development recognizes the importance of *liveable cities* by building social equity and inclusion through community-based, socially-engaged neighborhoods that include a vibrant arts ecology.[xxx]

Heritage: Buildings, architectural designs, and public art that depict historical persons and transition into contemporary design is influenced by both artists and architects. The creative techniques employed bridge each other's creative talents and should be considered local assets.

Quality of life: The quality of life offered by *place* is often associated with the presence of a *cultural district* where artistic studios, galleries, music or theatrical performances, ethnic food, and local/global cultures are clustered with unique traditions, public artwork, and parks or other gathering places. Quality of life and contemporary conveniences are promoted in branding and marketing materials to attract tourists, residents, businesses, and business relocation.

Competitive advantage: When looking to attract tourists, residents, or businesses, municipalities identify and promote what differentiates them from other locales. Audiences often seek venues, events or places that exhibit unique, quality, or timely experiences with heritage-oriented origins when deciding where to visit or attend.

Planning: Arts organization leaders should be considered an important resource. They have direct access to artists' needs, barriers, and considerations and can facilitate authentic and unique artistic content in your community. Work with all stakeholders within municipal and community planning initiatives to build strategic, mutually-beneficial tourism, economic development, and arts sector partnerships.

Events / New initiatives: Whether community-driven or for commercial gain, explore creative ways to generate support from other stakeholders through planning, long-term visioning, financial commitments, matching-fund leveraging (three-way business/arts sector partnerships), marketing support, and other means. Develop relationships that draw interest toward the membership of the arts community to maximize local arts sector input.

Reputation / Traditions: Municipal councils can take risks that develop their economies in new ways or focus on conservative, historical, and traditional economic drivers. Maintaining the status quo might be looked upon as a limiting factor—or as a unique advantage. Work together to find balance in the evolution of your community. Engage arts ecosystem stakeholders for input and ideas, ensuring all voices are heard.

Businesses have a unique position in the local arts ecosystem; they are often established locally and are rooted in their community, while some reach national or global markets and seek opportunities to grow their customer base. Interestingly, arts sector producers and venues gather a customer base: audiences. Finding common ground that benefits each stakeholder is the sweet spot!

Promotion of place: Businesses promote their locations to attract business clients and potential employees (ex-pats and new immigrants). They often draw upon quality of life assets outlined (See Artistic Driver #2: Place, *Municipality*).

Rooted to community: A business can influence the value of the arts within a community through their ties to place and, particularly, their customer base. Companies that support or make investments in local organizations, artists, arts events, or social initiatives contribute to a healthy community. Customers favor local businesses that (outwardly and proactively) give back to their community, showing their reciprocity through their purchasing power.

Creative thinking (influence): Broad-minded viewpoints and solutions-oriented intellect are highly desirable in business environments. These characteristics are an offshoot of arts sector engagement within creative environments. (See Artistic Driver #1: Creative Works, *Community Engagement.*)

Staff retention: An organizational culture that values creative thinking, inclusion, and teamwork often prioritizes staff involvement in community and artistic activities, perhaps linked to their company's corporate social responsibility program. (See Artistic Driver #1: *Creative Works, Business*.) A positive organizational culture attracts and retains staff resulting in less staff turnover, fewer training costs, consistent customer service, and retention of historical corporate knowledge.

Government

Provincial or state governments act as catalysts for arts sector development and growth. Whether through attraction incentives or development initiatives, they play an important role in keeping barriers to entry low and opportunity high for artists and the arts ecosystem. The province or state is often a significant player in larger projects that require multiple funding partners.

Quality of life: The same components as stated under *Municipalities* apply to provincial or state governments when considering cultural district enhancement or development. Quality of life and contemporary conveniences are promoted in branding and marketing materials to attract tourists, residents, businesses, and business relocation.

Provincial or state branding: An artist's creative output translates into a vibrant community; this vibrancy is often incorporated into promotional and branding initiatives. Arts leaders are important resources to assist provincial/state and community leaders in discovering authentic, unique, and artistic content that can strategically benefit tourism, economics, and arts sector development, and, increasingly, promote social impacts.

Capacity building: Developing partnerships with and working directly with arts sector leaders, government gains knowledge of the needs, gaps, and opportunities to build capacity within the arts sector. Informed civil staff and politicians builds capacity and overall sector sustainability for long-term societal, creative, and economic returns.

Events / Established initiatives: Have a conversation with arts sector administrators to identify creative support mechanisms through planning, long-term visioning, financial commitments, matching-fund programs, marketing support, and other means. Build upon prior successes, create new initiatives, cross-pollinate between sectors or provincial/state departments. Work with arts sector leaders, those who support the creative development of artists, especially those who work directly with artists!

Case Study: *Art In The Open*, Establishing a
Contemporary Arts Festival

*RE: FEAR OF THE UNKNOWN versus POSITIVE EXPERIENCE
BREEDS ENGAGEMENT*

When establishing a new program or a new event, you will
always encounter nay-sayers and skeptics. This story shows how
one person went from skeptic to enthusiast, breaking their own
pre-conceived ideas and barriers in the process.

In 2011, a new one-day contemporary visual arts festival, Art In
The Open, was initiated in downtown streets and public parks of
Charlottetown, Prince Edward Island (population 36,000). Led by
a professional contemporary artist and a professional art gallery
curator, they partnered with arts organizations, artists,
architects, community volunteers, and the municipality—all of
whom contributed time and resources to support the public art
project. As project liaison, I worked with municipal staff to
ensure the festival's needs and resource gaps were met and
risks were addressed.

When learning a 21-concurrent-fire art installation was part of
the event, a park manager seemed somewhat panicked. Some
statements the park manager uttered included (I paraphrase
here): "Artists are crazy!" "You can't trust [artists]!" "This is
insane!" "[The artists] just might burn down the park!" I assured
park staff the fire department was aware of the art installation
and the artist was taking appropriate safety precautions during
set up and burning activities. I communicated that fires would
not be lit should winds rise above a pre-determined speed (20
km/hour), as agreed with festival organizers.

The inaugural festival was an absolute success! There were no instances of abuse to art installations, people, parks, or outdoor spaces. The fire installation was reported as "magical" by residents and politicians the following day in the local newspaper. (The City of Charlottetown has since purchased this art piece.)

In 2012, the same organizers and partners came together for the second (now annual) contemporary outdoor art festival. The same park manager, now familiar with the festival and the organizers, enthusiastically greeted me (his now-familiar contact) with, "What are we doing this year?", rubbing his hands with earnest excitement and wearing a big smile of anticipation.

He was no longer hesitant to work with of a group of people with whom, before the inaugural event, he had limited engagement. His self-imposed barriers were replaced with enthusiasm after this (one) positive experience. His participation in future art activities is unknown, but the door is now open and his willingness to engage has expanded. His comfort zone within the arts milieu increased as an art event participant, organizer, and partner!

Artistic Driver #3: Linkages to the Arts Ecosystem

This section provides examples of potential (or anticipated) interactions between artists and primary ecosystem stakeholders. Some interactions relate to specific functionalities within the arts and cultural sector, therefore do not apply to all stakeholders. The lists that follow under each sub-category identify potential partners that are neither **exclusive** nor **all-inclusive** to that category.

Information provided in this section applies to both arts-centric and non-arts-centric stakeholders and suggests cross-collaboration opportunities. Think about other stakeholders from your own community not outlined here and add them to these lists.

Consider how these entities are linked to artists, core artistic creators, across all disciplines:

- Artists themselves: artists from across various disciplines associate frequently with one another.
- Producers: associated with theatre, music, dance, film, literature, festivals, and other modes of presentation. This may include curators in galleries and other such persons involved in the arts.
- Venues: management, technicians, staff, volunteers (including Boards of Directors), and other participants at galleries, bars, performance spaces, studios, and other locations.
- Funders: arts organizations, philanthropists, business, federal/provincial/state/ municipal governments,

politicians and representative staff, foundations, private funders, and other sources.

- Arts organizations and Heritage and Museum entities: arts councils, writer's guilds, craft councils, libraries, museums, heritage sites, theatre companies, and other groups and sites.
- Agents / Managers: anyone who directly manages an artist's career, tour, or an artist's catalogue of work, or other elements of their career; may include publicists.
- Audience: the general public, guests at private receptions, conference delegates, and others who view or otherwise witness artistic work.
- Community: supply outlets, community groups, churches, after-school programs, resident care facilities, community arts organizations, and other groups that link to artists and their works.
- Business: retail interaction, affordable rental arrangements through landlord partnerships, and/or philanthropy, or actions supporting their corporate social responsibility goals.

An ever-increasing linkage within the arts ecosystem is technology. Before 2020, the arts were in a transitional and disruptive period of technology integration and evolution. With the emergence of the COVID-19 pandemic in 2020, social and physical distancing measures put in place in response to this crisis have vigorously accelerated digital adaptation worldwide for artists, arts organizations, governments, business, and the general public. With an eye to traditional art forms or hybrid traditional/digital art forms, an anticipated need for a new creative intermediary is forming in whispers within the ecosystem. This suggested intermediary would link an artist to a (human) technologist to both support the artist's original art form and facilitate inclusion, adaptation and/or distribution of their work to digital applications. This person (or entity) is thought to hold in-depth understanding of technology along with respect and knowledge of the value of traditional art forms. They are assumed to work as a partner or co-creator within the *artists'* creative process, ensuring neither traditional art forms nor artists with limited technological capacity are abandoned during this highly transformative period in our history and the sector's evolution. This, creative, partner-like intermediary is (mostly) conceptual. Outside of the artist/technologist creative partnership mentioned, technologically-based gaps exist for some artists', tied to online marketing and promotional requirements for relevancy adapted to the digital world; solutions are often bridged from within an artist's personal networks or via self-directed learning.

Artificial intelligence (AI) is another form of technology seeping into the world of art. Although I don't venture into this topic here, many reputable sources are available that delve into multi-faceted applications of AI associated with the arts sector. An excellent portal for insight into how the arts sector in Canada is harnessing AI is the Canadian Association for the Performing Arts[xxxi] (CAPACOA) and their associated partners and projects.

In the following groupings of stakeholders, I list potential points of interaction that support local partnership-building opportunity through outlined linkages. You will note considerable overlap among stakeholders in some areas which suggests significant opportunity to explore win-win partnership options.

Arts Organizations

Arts organizations act as primary access points for non-arts-centric stakeholders to engage and partner with the arts sector and its creative riches. Arts leaders are positioned like the hub of a wheel, the primary point of receiving and sharing information for others' benefit, across sectors and networks. The list below details how arts organizations and their leaders can navigate within the centre of this hub.

Artists: Arts leaders are the connectors with and for artists through artistic disciplines, programming, funding disbursement, new initiatives, memberships, and other means.

Venues (their own and others): Arts leaders provide spaces for presentation of creative works that intermingle management, technicians, staff, volunteers, artist networks, funders, businesses, and the general public.

Agents: Arts organizations build relationships with other intermediaries who directly manage or promote an artist's career or artwork. This group includes publicists, tour managers, publishing agents and others; each holds a specific role that might include working on behalf of their client (artist) to promote their client's work or secure gigs, or perhaps working to obtain artistic works for film, television and other commercial uses, working through the artist's agent. Relationships intersect and intertwine continuously; the multi-functionality of an arts organization demands leadership that can fluidly and effectively navigate partnerships and opportunities for artists at every turn.

Media: Arts organization leaders or appointed staff are often the primary contact between broadcasters, print media, publications, social media campaigns, and other forms of media and the artist. They tell the stories of their own organization and may also act as promoter for artists and their work.

Audience: The whole of an arts organization takes on a public relations role with patrons, the general public, business contacts, government partners and through private receptions, conferences, and other consumers of creative works. Your audience goes beyond those who attend your events or sit in your venue's seats. Good public relations are everyone's responsibility, not only the organization's management or appointed spokesperson.

Provincial/state/national networks: Arts organization leaders often represent the arts within peer networks provincially, at the state level, or nationally—across programs, councils, task forces, and other assemblies.

Arts and heritage organizations: Representatives of arts organizations often sit as a board or committee member or colleague of arts councils, libraries, museums, arts venues, and similar organizations.

Cultural industries (producers and staff): Arts organizations may work directly with film and television production teams, sound/music recording colleagues, festivals, book publishers, digital media experts, architects, fashion industry representatives, and mass production and distribution firms. A senior administrator or manager with a role or knowledge of specific subject matter is often the contact within an arts organization.

> *Author's Note*: Cultural industries have often referred to arts-centric industry while creative industries referred to other industries not specifically related to the arts sector or artistic creation. It has become more common for the term 'creative industries' to refer to the category including film, publishers and such while 'creative economy' encapsulates non-arts-centric stakeholders. I use 'creative industries' to include noted stakeholders.

Creative industries (producers and staff): Arts organizations use the technology and services of graphic design, advertising, technological design (such as AI, augmented reality, or virtual reality), software design, industrial design, and other creative industry suppliers. Incorporating digital and other creative industry services and applications might fall to a senior administrator or someone knowledgeable in associated applications who represents their organization.

Funders / Partners: It is most often senior administrators or associated managers (in larger arts organizations) who work directly with federal and provincial/state government politicians and staff, other arts organizations, philanthropists, foundations, private funders, business leaders, and other funding sources.

Community: With heightened awareness of the social impacts of arts participation, arts organizations are well positioned to work closely with community groups, immigrants, churches, and other arts organizations. The arts organization's leader is often the point person in these relationships.

Tourists: As a response to creativity and artwork production, tourists might flock to see, experience, touch, and embrace multiple facets of local culture. Who does your community attract? Why? What stories and creative assets remain under the radar? Arts organizations and their leadership are positioned to facilitate partnerships between tourism industry professionals and creative content presenters such as artisans, theatres, fringe festivals, musicians, writers, and others who want to link their work to the tourism sector.

Heritage and Museums

This important stakeholder in the arts ecosystem links between past and present-day realities, traditions, and the many layers of community traditions, stories, industries and more.

Historical: By looking back in time, heritage and museums tell the story of your community through a multiplicity of storylines, geographies, and personalities. Artists are often called upon to enact these stories such as through character role-plays, songs, or stories.

Community: As a community organization member, heritage and museums filters into community groups, churches, arts organizations, and other entities. Heritage and museums can play a dual role linking both supporting community organizations' programming and presenting heritage programming to community organization memberships.

Venues (their own and others): By highlighting and exposing the past and present, heritage and museums connect venues through management, technicians, staff, volunteers, and artist networks. Historical and museum venues develop ongoing programming in association with internal and external constituents, research, and special events.

Tourists: In response to unique historical contexts promoted by heritage and museums, tourists seek ways to see, experience, touch, and embrace multiple and various aspects of local, past, and present heritage.

Residents: Residents are audience members who support programming as architect and heritage enthusiasts, guests at private receptions, conference delegates, and arts ecosystem participants in other ways.

Artists: Artistic disciplines can intersect in heritage and museum spaces, although primarily as the creators of work displayed in the space or as musicians and performers.

Provincial/state/national networks: Heritage and museums often have representation within a peer network, provincially, at the state level, or nationally across programs, councils, task forces, and other entities involved in strategic planning.

Funders / Partners: Heritage and museum organizations work directly with, and are often an arm of, federal and provincial/state governments. Staff work with politicians, arts organizations, philanthropists, foundations, private funders, business leaders, and community groups to build support for and market their programming.

Arts and (other) heritage and museum organizations: Leaders of arts, heritage, and museum organizations often sit as board and committee members or colleagues of arts councils, libraries, museums, municipal planning groups, and arts venues.

Media: Heritage organizations and museums are often the primary storyteller for distributing their media content. They tell stories of their own organization, their programming, and artists' work as it links to their programming.

Cultural / Creative industries (producers and staff): Heritage and museum organizations often work with film/television production teams and publishers with limited interaction through sound/music recording, festivals, digital media, architects, fashion industry, and other aspects of the production of artistic creative works. In this period of disruption, along with interests of heritage and museum properties to attract larger audiences, opportunities to integrate many aspects of cultural industries into on-site production and presentation offerings are varied and abundant.

Residents

The general public intersects with the arts ecosystem through numerous access points, with varying degrees of separation between these access points and artists. The ability to speak with or work directly with an artist can be a meaningful incentive for non-art-centric stakeholders to partner or volunteer with an arts organization or project. The points of access are:

Venues: Through management, technicians, staff, volunteers, and other roles.

Cultural industries staff: Through film/television production, sound/music recording, festivals, book publishing, digital media, mass production and distribution, architecture, fashion events, and other means.

Creative industries staff: Through graphic design firms, advertising firms, technological design [AI, augmented reality, virtual reality], software design, and industrial design staff.

Arts and (other) heritage and museum organizations: Through membership or serving on the boards of arts councils, libraries, museums, arts venues, and other organizations.

Non-arts sector entities: Through involvement and participation in community group projects and organizations, healthcare facilities, educational programs, and other activities mounted by these entities.

Business: Through business owners and their staff, business service organizations, and similar business-oriented organizations (for example, arts/business incubators, hubs, and accelerators).

Media: Through print media (opinion pieces) and social media, residents can engage directly with artists. Social media accounts are often managed personally by the artist and have become an important engagement portal for fans, online funding campaign participants, clients (who purchase from the artist), and are used by artists for self-promotion purposes.

Artists: Through their public-facing art studios, public
performances, backstage passes, and festivals; direct interaction
between artists and the public is often limited.

Funders / Partners: Through municipal or
federal/provincial/state governments, public servants process
sponsorships, grant applications, and funding agreements;
political ministers or political appointees often meet artists and
arts organization leaders through photo opportunities or arts
sector lobby efforts.

Tourists: Through word of mouth, residents have the power to
influence tourists' engagement with local arts and cultural
offerings, including social media recommendations. The closer a
resident's connection to the sector, the greater impact their
recommendations have on the sector (and artists) overall.

Municipality

Political leaders who are local champions for the arts are a
strong asset for the sector. But research noted in this book
identified the value of creativity and organic development sits at
the grass-roots level of the sector. This value placement is in
contrast with structured institutional development which is top-
down or hierarchal. Municipal governments and their appointed
committees should facilitate, not expect to lead, arts sector
development and growth; they are a catalyst to support art-
centric initiatives. A top-down approach by government to
direct or meet pre-determined targets sets limits to creative
outcomes while a bottom-up or grass roots approach stimulates
unlimited possibilities.

Finding the sweet spot where both an institutional approach for expected outcomes and the boundless approach of creativity co-exist is a worthwhile challenge. It requires administrations to forfeit an element of control while trusting in the process and people in place. Taking a calculated risk that ventures into uncharted territory opens the door to new, unexpected impacts and results on which to build. (See case study *Open House* at the end of Chapter 7.)

Artists / Core cultural producers (all disciplines): The intersection between artists and city council/staff is often limited. Establish relationships with arts organizations for inclusive opportunities to draw from the creativity pool of local arts community resources for several creative and artistic applications, programming, or long-term planning initiatives.

Venues: Politicians and municipal staff often work with arts organization and festival management, technicians, staff, and associated volunteers. Intersection with artists might include sponsorship events or public receptions. Arts sector leaders are a resource for knowledge about arts-centric initiatives in development but not yet in public view and may add value across sectors, festivals, or other initiatives.

Arts and heritage and museum organizations: Politicians and municipal staff might be members of arts councils, libraries, museums, arts venues, and other entities. Their involvement informs them of arts and organization-specific knowledge; alternatively, they share knowledge and insights of municipal processes or opportunities, creating a bridge to arts sector organizations.

Cultural / Creative industries (producers and staff): Partnered opportunities may be rare, depending on political portfolios, however, politicians and municipal staff may intersect with film/television production teams, sound/music recording contacts, festivals organizers, and associated stakeholders. Municipalities may intersect with cultural and creative industry partners through zoning and legislation or regulations that pertain to associated initiatives. Economic development initiatives may seek to attract film and television productions, as well as online gaming corporations who employ a variety of creators such as animation professionals.

Funders / Partners: Through grant programs, multi-partner, financial support programs and other initiatives, politicians and municipal staff work directly with federal and provincial/state governments. They may also associate with philanthropists, foundations, private funders, and business leaders through multi-level government and private sector partnerships.

Media: The media is often directed by one municipal staff member. Joint announcements with community and arts sector partners are an opportunity for the municipality to publicly link and champion their support of arts sector initiatives.

Agents: Municipalities often have limited access to anyone who directly manages an artist's career or artwork. Exceptions might include commissioned artwork, projects that hire artists to demonstrate or present their artistic creative work, or previously noted board memberships.

Audience: Politicians' public spotlight provides them access to arts sector activities that may be associated with the general public, private receptions, conferences, and other events. This is a great opportunity to champion their support for the arts, arts programs, and subsequent partnerships.

Community: Similar to general audience populations, politicians' public spotlight affords them recognition and access to arts sector activities that might be associated with community groups, immigrants, churches, arts organizations, and other community sectors. This access might also be an opportunity to bridge community inclusion through the arts, realizing access to and participation in the arts builds community.

Tourists: It is often a councilor or the mayor who acts as a spokesperson to encourage tourism engagement with festivals, events, heritage recognition, and other arts affiliations or who gains access to artists at special events.

Business / Entrepreneurs: Municipalities encourage business development. Linkage to the arts ecosystem is often between business owners and staff at business and arts service organizations, and entities that offer support to arts entrepreneurs such as arts incubators and accelerators. Developing policy, programs and opportunities that bridge partnerships among all stakeholders is a holistic approach that encourages a strong local economy.

Business

As noted, businesses have a unique link to the local arts ecosystem. They are often established locally and rooted in their community, while some have a national or global reach. Businesses are offered various opportunities to intersect with the arts ecosystem.

Patrons: A business can attract several customers from the arts ecosystem, depending on the product or service they offer to: artists, arts organizations, residents, other businesses, heritage and museum organizations, tourists, festival participants, conference delegates, and many others. Strong business/client relationships can lead to successful, long-term partnerships.

Venues (their own and others): If businesses want to partner with arts organizations, they might consider investing in venues and organizations that offer unique programming, celebratory events, and social impact partnership opportunities. Access to venues and programming is often through arts organization's management, technicians, staff, and volunteers.

Community sponsorship and in-kind support: Business and partnership opportunities abound through arts organizations, community groups, immigrant associations, churches, and other entities that support and promote the arts. One option is engaging through corporate social responsibility initiatives, particularly valuable to discover gap areas through consultation with arts organizations. Consider developing a unique partnership offering to benefit participating stakeholders.

Creative industries (producers and staff): Depending on the line of business, spinoff benefits often accrue from film/television production, sound/music publishing, and festivals produced in your community. Some businesses act as local suppliers for film and television productions such as carpentry, electrical or any number of movie-set or sound stage supplies. *A broader link to the arts community might incorporate* creative talent of local artists in elements of business promotion, in public spaces such as parks and malls, or through ambassador roles that represent the community. Some examples might include promotional and design planning for new programs in addition to graphic design, advertising, technological design, software design, industrial design, and other elements of business promotion.

Government

As advised for municipalities, provincial or state governments should facilitate, but not lead, arts sector development and growth. Government partners are an important catalyst that support art-centric initiatives; however, a top-down approach sets limitations to creative outcomes. Bottom-up or grass-roots approaches tend to stimulate unexpected and beneficial results. It is a worthwhile challenge to cede some level of control, therefore not limiting artists' creativity.

Artists / Core cultural producers (all disciplines): The intersection between artists and provincial/state department staff is limited. Established relationships with arts organizations increase opportunities to utilize and promote the creativity of local arts community resources.

Venues: Events and venues are often a primary point of intersection for politicians and their staff with artists. Through receptions and grant or funding activities, arts organizations and festival management are the link to artists.

Arts and (other) heritage and museum organizations:
Politicians and provincial/state government staff can participate
as members of arts councils, libraries, museums, performance
venues, theatre troupes, arts presenting/artist-run
organizations, and arts training through funding programs and
institutions that support the arts.

Cultural / Creative industries (producers and staff): Politicians
often have limited direct interaction with graphic design firms,
advertising firms, technological design [AI, augmented reality,
virtual reality], software design, and industrial design, but they
may indirectly intersect with artists or arts organizations
through industry stimulus programs and other funding
envelopes. Politicians and their staff may intersect with
film/television production teams, music industry contacts,
festivals organizers, and associated stakeholders through
funding initiatives that promote and support creative industries.

Funders / Partners: Through their work, multiple levels of
government, politicians and their staff may, occasionally,
associate with philanthropists, foundations, private funders, and
business leaders through arts sector initiatives and partnerships.
Many funding programs require financial partnerships with two
or more arts and community organizations or levels of
government.

Media: Working through one or more staff members, joint
announcements are an opportunity to both support and
promote arts sector initiatives. Consider including arts
organizations and artists in these publicity events to profile the
artists and champion their work.

Agents: Politicians and government staff often have limited access to anyone who directly manages an artist's career or their creative works. Arts advocacy groups that lobby government and arts organization leaders who present to standing committees are the most common connection to the arts ecosystem.

Audience: As noted, politicians' public spotlight provides access to arts sector activities that may be associated with the general public, private receptions, conference, and other events. These public appearances offer a significant opportunity to champion the arts to broad audiences.

Community: Community groups, immigrants, churches, arts organizations, and events in the community present opportunity for politicians to publicly access arts sector activities, which are tied to their political role. Consider incorporating arts disciplines as a gateway to important discussions regarding local, national, or international issues.

Tourists: This linkage to the arts ecosystem often falls to a political leader or their appointee, a spokesperson who encourages tourism engagement and promotes arts sector programming. Some large events encourage tourism and give politicians and their staff access to artists at special events. Promote artists and recognize their work through paid appearances within integrated marketing plans that support local, provincial/state, or national tourism initiatives.

Business / Entrepreneurs: Government has linkages to business owners and staff, and arts service organizations. These business owners, managers and organizations may include artists, artist cooperatives, artist-run centers, and associated partners.

Artistic Driver #4: Non-Financial Resources

Artists' creativity and intellect are stimulated through multiple sources. Their stimuli might include personal relationships, a geographic location, like-minded people and peers, critical observation of politics, or everyday storylines that generate their creative capital. Inputs vary and are unique to each artist.

Professional networks are conduits to other artists and offer opportunity for artistic and creative growth. Whether through artist-in-resident programs, discipline-specific courses, workshops, or mentorships, these training elements provide critical professional development for artists to advance in their profession.

Physical infrastructure, including arts organizations, supports many forms of artistic production and presentation. Equally important are partnerships and relationships associated with these entities. What functions as supportive infrastructure includes many intersecting points outlined in this book, as particularly noted within the section *Artistic Driver #3: Linkages to the Arts Ecosystem*.

Resources for artistic creation are varied and unique, such as recycled items, and materials are often sourced locally. These raw materials must be easy to access and available in sufficient abundance. Resources could range from seaweed to a precise type of ash, from discarded pieces of wood or car parts to running water, or from paint supplies and digital technology to musicians, dancers, and actors. The list is endless.

Locally-sourced materials also lead to sustainability outcomes as artists' environmental impacts are minimal, leaving a small carbon footprint. Purchasing, hiring, or otherwise using local resources supports the local economy and those who work within it. In this way, artists have a positive impact on their local environment and their community; they generally reinvest in where they live as opposed to outside their community.

The following information provides insight as to how other primary stakeholders can support the ecosystem and intersect with artists via non-financial resources, the fourth artistic driver.

Arts Organizations

Value: Increase your organization's value to your patrons, artists, residents, and your professional networks (local, regional, and national). Engage with interactive participation through creative programming or benefits to your stakeholders.

Mystique: People not involved in the arts sector are often curious (yet unaware) of how creative artworks evolve, whether backstage, in a recording booth, or in an artist's studio. Take this opportunity to engage stakeholders' curiosity for a 'peek behind the veil' in all aspects of operations. *This unique and strategic resource can be leveraged in many forms!*

Mentorship: Share skills and knowledge through educational and mentorship programs; cross-train staff to work in various positions, building capacity in your organization; and leverage your staff's expertise by developing leadership opportunities for junior staff.

Common voice: Become the trusted voice for the cultural sector, working with and on behalf of artists, arts organizations, funders, political leaders, community groups, and businesses.

Advocacy: Evidence-based data, that is information based on sound research, helps in advocacy efforts. Use public findings such as national, regional, or municipal statistics on the economic, social, and health impacts of the arts ecosystem. Additionally, develop the means to generate information (data) from within your own organization that describes quantifiable growth (for example, numbers of patrons, increased revenues, and/or numbers of subscribers, visitors, volunteers, partners, and sponsors) to support new initiatives in which you seek to invest or attract investors. Communicate these findings through stories and by talking about the impacts that the data indicate; this helps attract interest and support at the local level. Non-arts-centric stakeholders appreciate this data-driven approach; an added benefit is that data build a perception of value and return on investment for your organization.

An excellent advocacy tool that highlights qualitative impacts of the arts is Americans for the Arts *Social Impact + Arts* interactive explorer. A link to this tool is provided on my website's *News & Resources* page and in the reference section of this book.

Heritage and Museums

Community connectivity: These facilities and the knowledge they hold are sought after resources, particularly by residents and tourists. Their local knowledge, stories, and artifacts are of interest to historians and those wanting to trace their personal heritage.

Networks: These organizations are often linked to other local, regional, and national networks. Knowledge, information sharing, and promotional opportunities are valuable resources to tap into that can positively influence specific, desired outcomes.

Space: Working with those who manage these entities to develop arts and cultural presentations or partnerships are a great fit to mutually support programming objectives and create sustainable operations.

Residents

Residents are a significant local resource that both support and drive demand for a creative, innovative society. Consider ways and means to invite residents to share and participate in your organization or event as a valued community member.

Volunteers: Residents offer their expertise through serving on boards, participating in events, and acting as program presenters or volunteers. This group of generous humans and their word of mouth testimonials (and social media postings) about your organization are critically important resources (and assets) you possess.

Connect through arts organizations: It is through this porthole to the arts sector that residents gain their *access point* to give through volunteer services, as staff or donors (tangible or monetary), as a mentor, or by contributing through community strategic planning sessions.

Strategic media campaigns: Interactive activities or media campaigns that generate public interest are especially effective. Give your audience a *call to action* within your publicity campaign. Through the media, invite residents' input for naming a festival or perhaps a new program. Make a contest out of it by offering a prize from your organization. This prize need not cost you financially; perhaps it is an experience, free tickets, a tour, a meet-and-greet, or another asset you have access to through your organization or established partnerships.

Building relationships through these connections are important to an arts organization's long-term sustainability. Develop a long-term plan to move your patrons to new levels of engagement, carefully managing the relationship and their increasing value to your organization. From their initial curiosity and participation in a transactional activity, then through multiple steps along the value chain to advocacy, this is *relationship marketing.*[xxxii]Success is heavily weighted toward *genuine* interest in, appreciation for, and support of your colleagues, patrons, partners and others.

Municipality

Community connection: The municipal stakeholder connects or links to funding, community organizations, professional networks (locally, regionally, and nationally), schools and education programs, and residents. Investigate the points of intersection that have significant potential for mutual benefits among multiple stakeholders and leverage that intersectionality as a common point of interest, a starting point to discuss non-financial resource sharing and potential partnerships.

Community outreach: When excellent relationships exist, it is possible to piggy-back—build upon established groundwork—on your partner's promotional and marketing outreach at no cost. Or work out a deal with community media publishers, perhaps establishing a preferred rate for a period of time or for specified longer term conditions. *Taking advantage of a potential opportunity is key; having a trusted relationship is a must.*

Bridge the cultural sector: Be a trusted voice for your arts organization, educating municipal stakeholders of sector activities while being a point of contact to find solutions to issues that hinder cultural entrepreneurs. Build your profile as the connector, the hub point that works on others' behalf; for example, addressing municipal bylaws regarding signage, parking, hours of operation, and other regulatory or legislative barriers on behalf of arts-centric entrepreneurs or festivals.

Building community: Opportunities for cross-collaboration between artists and municipalities are everywhere. Some artists are highly skilled outside of their chosen discipline; others hold superior acting, engagement, and presentation skills. Hiring

artists to fill gaps through short-term, contract work supports
the gig economy in which they work. Introducing this discussion
most likely falls to local arts service organization leadership,
such as an arts council or cultural human resources council
(CHRC). This idea might also find relevancy at the national CHRC
level.

Commissioned work: Hire an artist for commissioned work.
Keep the opportunity local to value grass-roots artistry. Besides
working with a local artist, artworks may incorporate a local
context that grounds its authenticity to a specific place or
geography. Work might be commissioned as a gift, to
commemorate a specific occasion, or to be presented as public
art.

Cultural mapping: Municipalities might consider developing and
managing (or contributing financial resources to) an open
source mapping tool that presents and connects the local arts
ecosystem through one resource. Remote areas might consider
regional mapping initiatives. This tool can be used in
collaboration with arts programming, tourism associations,
business organizations (chambers of commerce), and economic
development initiatives.

Business

Employees: Employees are a business's greatest resource.
Corporate social responsibility programs leverage staff for
community good, with a secondary positive impact on
employees by symbolizing their value, importance, and
appreciation in the eyes of their employer.

Consumption: Businesses and their employees both consume artwork and benefit from its creation. Depending on the business, the benefit to a business might include a higher number of patrons dining before or after a performance or acting as the supplier for materials to create a public stage or individual artwork. When local residents purchase tickets or artworks, they maximize revenue returns to the artist either directly or through a local intermediary.

Building community: If your business has access to unused space, transforming an empty office space into an art studio is a highly valued asset to artists; natural light is an important factor for visual artists. Short-term work contracts between artists and business are an ideal way for each partner to adapt to each other's environment, to ascertain each other's qualities, and investigate other synergetic characteristics. Contract work might be highly appealing to artists if it is creative, and a means to supplement their income between artistic projects.

Commissioned work: Seek opportunities to hire an artist, to commission their work. Keeping the resource local promotes the value of artistic presence in your community; be a champion for the arts. Some works may be a gift, an award, a uniquely branded item, or commemorate a specific occasion. If you are a retailer, consider offering series of works for sale from different local artists.

Innovation: Artists have intuitively creative minds. Consider them as creative consultants to partner with during meetings or brainstorming sessions. Ask an arts organization to recommend local artists who hold desired facilitation and visioning skills or specific content knowledge. Organize a meeting in advance or employ an on-site facilitator to connect the artist into what is probably an unfamiliar business environment.

Government

Tourism and cultural departments: Encourage government staff to seek opportunities to work in partnership with arts organizations and artists. Focus objectives on building both awareness of the arts sector and long-term relationships that support mutually beneficial goals and values across multiple sectors.

Community / Arms-length government agencies: Seek opportunities to work in partnership with arts organizations and artists that support mutually beneficial goals and values. Consider sharing resources and assets, cross-promotional initiatives, partnered programming, and other options.

Innovation departments: As suggested for *Business* in this section, consider artists as creative consultants with whom to work during meetings or brainstorming sessions. Work with local arts councils to identify artists who possess necessary facilitation and visioning skills or specific content knowledge. Organize a meeting in advance or employ an on-site facilitator to ensure a comfort level for the artist in an institutionalized government environment.

Skills-based training: Invest in artists' creative development by supporting discipline-specific training opportunities through local, regional, national, or international programs. Creativity is an artist's core skill that, like any skill, requires nurturing and exploration in search of excellence. Work in partnership with arts organizations to assure programs align with local arts sector needs, opportunities, gaps, and weaknesses. Better yet, ensure a mechanism is in place for the sector's grass roots to inform government on a regular basis regarding programs or policy that intend to address current and anticipated sector needs.

Research: Engage the arts sector in primary research initiatives, gathering data directly from or related to their membership. Proactively share arts sector research downstream with arts sector organizations and other non-arts-centric ecosystem stakeholders. Evidence-based research on the arts—quantitative and qualitative—has become prevalent at the national level in Canada; research at the local level is often limited to quantitative results linked to economic impacts or singular operations. Activate research initiatives that support local arts ecosystem stakeholders and align with national initiatives to inform and advance sector development at the local level.

Artistic Driver #5: Visioning

A vision, shared among ecosystem stakeholders, is critical to attain holistic results.

Visioning is often associated with strategic planning exercises within an institution or at a municipal level where input from stakeholders, community, and residents are gathered through surveys, open house events, or public consultations. I expand this narrative when I suggest a vision should be shared among (and planned within) a group of organizations who either contribute to or are affected by the results of such planning. Think of planning that occurs within a cooperative or alliance framework that includes *other sector* (non-arts-centric) participants.

This concept relates directly to next-generation cultural sector planning that reflects social equity, diversity, and inclusion measures broader than one sector. This concept also closes the power distance relationship gap between decision makers and those often with the least power (usually the artists) to speak directly to decision makers about their concerns and how another's decision will affect their livelihood.

In arts sector planning, a shared vision starts with arts sector stakeholders participating in alliance discussions. The group comprises sector leaders representing their organizations and memberships. Participants bring their own priorities to the discussion while remaining open to initiatives that mutually support both their own and other primary arts ecosystem stakeholders' planning efforts. Coming together to investigate these opportunities, the participants explore mutually-beneficial multi-sector partnerships, expand their visions to a holistic view, and generate a web of support that extends to all ecosystem stakeholders.

The challenge is finding time and willing participants.

Stakeholders must see the value in this process. Some would-be participants require a response to "What's in it for me?" to commit, while others might be guarded in sharing corporate knowledge. Strong leadership must initiate, facilitate, and manage initial discussions and *long-term* commitments.

Visioning is a forum for communication and planning between stakeholders. In this model, everyone contributes to the work with the expectation of improved shared outcomes to individual sectors, organizations, residents, and grass-roots contributors.

What is the artist's place in visioning?

Stepping back from the big picture and refocusing on the grass-roots perspective, artists possess intuitive and longtail views and insights about place. They are acutely aware if their values, intentions, and skills align with the underlying local culture—or not. Some elements of place perceived as complementary to an artist's presence include a knowledge-based environment and access to like-minded professionals, peers, and muses to spur artistic visioning. Connections to arts organizations and arts networks are valuable access points for artists to integrate into the local arts ecosystem.

Public support and engagement in an artist's work result from its presentation at arts organizations, promotional events, and through publications. Face-to-face engagement may occur at artists' studios or in arts hub locations, often with artists on-site and their work for sale.

In the past, cultural districts developed organically. It has become common practice for municipalities and business interests to lead cultural district development and evolution. How artists can afford to create when capital and development interests force costs upward, and force artists out of the cultural district they created, has become a common concern in the arts community. Mass exodus of artists will hollow out present-day creative nodes; municipalities and local neighborhoods need to adopt measures that allow artists some level of stability to maintain their presence. Losing artists will diminish attraction to cultural districts and communities, in turn reducing the vibrancy that sustains economic and social interests.

Once again, a long-term collective *vision* provides a roadmap to avoid the departure of core artistic creators from communities, supported by all ecosystem stakeholders. Once artists leave, authentic creativity dissipates, to be replaced by cookie-cutter offerings—artistic matter that carries limited original conception and is easily copied and rebuilt or transferred to multiple geographies through mass production. There is little attraction to, and few will be curious to explore, a place where elements that dictate sameness dominate. Artists and their artistic offerings organically add a unique vibe, colour, flair, and attraction that is anything but *the same*.

The lists that follow describe how to build a collective vision with stakeholders while advancing creative expression in arts organizations. It considers the operation of heritage sites and museums, the personal experiences of residents, municipal development initiatives, impacts on the business community, arts sector development, and overall socio-economic impacts.

Arts Organizations

Building awareness and reach: Consider utilizing local, regional, and national networks to build recognition of your organization's programming, impact, partnerships, successes, cultural offerings, and more.

Inclusion strategy: Address multilingual and other program considerations for newcomers and immigrant community members. Reflect on accessibility concerns for those with mobility, intellectual, or other-abled issues.

Community builder: Develop opportunities for artists, creators, ethno-cultural contributors, volunteers, and local stakeholders to connect with those outside of primary programming functions (e.g., build a community garden, participate in a neighborhood initiative, or partner with an organization or business that champions your work).

Creative works: Be a risk taker, a leader, with new creative works. Consider your organization's and community's tolerance for challenging the norm as you facilitate new works. Artists are not intimidated by blank canvasses; the challenge may be convincing funders, partners, sponsors, and Boards of Directors to explore new programming initiatives.

Socio-economics: Use your influence, assets, and unique resources to support and promote initiatives that link to creativity, social impacts, revenues for artists, and other socially and economically beneficial outcomes. Cross-sectoral and community partnerships tie well to socially focused outcomes.

Heritage and Museums

Partnerships: Link programming with local educational curriculum. Find year-round partners through shared knowledge generation and programming.

Cultural alliance: Establish membership within a cultural alliance formed by the arts sector. Use this opportunity to communicate knowledge and share resources that support participants' objectives and align with municipal and regional governments' backing.

Off-site programming: Consider rotating exhibitions in public spaces. Work with partners to promote each other's sites and programming, effectively cross-marketing off-site exhibitions to draw visitors to your central location. Consider programming at travel entry-points for tourists (airports, cruise ship ports, train stations, and other venues). Consider year-round and seasonal programming options to attract locals and tourists.

Outreach: Invite artists and arts organizations to display and perform at your site; invite these same stakeholders to bounce around ideas for mid- and long-term planning. Develop arts and heritage festivals, regionally and nationally, either solely or in partnership with others. Cross-promote and cross-pollinate resources and ideas through partners and local cultural sector stakeholders. Reach outside your traditional target market but first identify who or what that is.

Residents

Overall support: Invite input from local residents. This opportunity can increase residents' level of engagement, break down self-imposed barriers about the arts sector, and will promote personal creative development.

Creating thinking: A ripple effect of engagement and participation in the creative sector is increased self-expression, tolerance, team building, and problem-solving abilities. This impact is far-reaching for individuals and communities.

Municipality

Ten-Year timeline: Successful cultural planning moves outside of short-term political cycles to support consistency and sustainability within arts sector development. A ten-year timeline is recommended, realizing plans are not static and are reviewed annually to incorporate unforeseen opportunities and challenges. It is key to remain focused on the long-term vision; the road to get there is adaptable.

Resident engagement: Invite residents to cultural planning sessions to glean ideas from their interest and knowledge. Especially invite artists and arts organizations by working through member-based art groups and organizations to reach the artists. Find trusted voices in the arts sector to encourage artists' participation, or maybe offer two separate community consultations: one with the arts sector and another with residents.

Cultural district: Understand the value of cultural districts with a cautious eye to development, realizing forms of capital development, such as gentrification measures, that increase the cost of living can impede affordability for core artistic creators (artists). Understand and envision long-term results related to increased inequity upon the district. Use foresight to mitigate risks that may impede cultural district development, such as reduced vibrancy or hindered authentic expression that artists generate, or other off-shoots of organically developed cultural districts not easily replicated.

Cultural alliance: The local arts sector should spearhead a cultural alliance with representation from all disciplines of practice. Representatives of the alliance can then inform other community or municipal task forces or advisory councils with one consistent voice that represents many. Arts sector representation at any table is a gateway to two-way communication and resource sharing that addresses the sector's and a municipality's objectives.

Bylaws: Engaging representatives from the arts sector during planning sessions brings a sector-specific perspective that identifies the needs of arts sector retailers, festivals, and arts organizations. It considers multilingual, set up/tear down requirements, accessibility, and other priorities.

Liaison: Assign a facilitator and liaison role to a municipal staff member who will work directly with individual arts organizations (or artists) on specific initiatives. Within municipal operations, create internal, cross-departmental alliances with increased cultural intelligence, that is, competency in understanding the value of arts and cultural activities and their role in municipal objectives. Sharing such knowledge invites inclusion and buy-in from staff otherwise unengaged in the outcomes.

Inclusion strategy: Consider the needs of immigrants, artists, other-abled, and new residents in your marketing efforts and sales teams. Dovetail this with efforts to promote social, artistic, and cultural inclusion within your business and, by extension, to the community.

Rootedness: Become knowledgeable about local heritage, traditions, and the key players in your community. Consider how to strengthen ties to these elements by respecting their importance and actively embracing them to deepen your value within the community. Seek cross-sector relationships and partnerships with entities that share core values, which will attract a wider audience or customer base through partnered community initiatives.

Seek creativity: Seek immigrants, artists, or locals for their expertise and knowledge, particularly those who originate from other parts of the country or globally. Invite artistic contribution to your planning and team-building initiatives. Work through a member-based arts organization to find a good match of knowledge and facilitation skills for the desired task. These initiatives build good faith between your business and the arts community and can lead to greater partnerships, community integration, and perceived value in your community.

Technological expertise: If you are a technology enterprise, consider sharing your expertise with arts organizations through resource-sharing partnerships or other means that build win-win prospects.

Author's Note: Digitization of the arts is a timely topic with increased attention for the last few years, partially driven by granting agencies' support for arts sector stakeholders to align with technological developments and leverage these developments for the sector's advantage. I anticipate an ongoing and increasing number of collaborative opportunities for artists and arts organizations via this medium, especially following the explosion of online content and digital connectivity experienced during the global COVID-19 pandemic.

Expertise (generally): Encourage staff and business owners to share their areas of expertise with arts organizations to fill gaps that support the larger arts community ecosystem—as board members, volunteer support, and other roles. Business skillsets are highly valued such as legal, accounting, taxation, fundraising, and governance. Publicity and communications remain important contributions, however these skills are often available, more and more, among arts organization staff.

Government

Events / Established initiatives: Seek creative ways to support arts sector stakeholders through their inclusion in planning, long-term visioning, and government commitments to financial resources, matching-fund programs, and marketing support. Build upon established events/initiatives to form new initiatives or facilitate partner initiatives with other sectors and provincial/state departments. Similar to municipal governments, create internal, cross-departmental alliances that support the arts from different perspectives (e.g., economic, culture, heritage, health, social services, and other areas).

Business and creative development: Support artists' needs and gaps, considering the increasing need for business, marketing, technology, and communication skills that sustain an artistic practice through online and face-to-face contact. Invite input from artists and grass-roots stakeholders to inform policy and programs from their perspective.

Linkages to tourism products: Develop programs and resources that dovetail tourism and arts sector stakeholders; encourage cultivation of mutually-beneficial opportunities for artists, arts organizations, and tourists through initiatives that meet government objectives.

Immigration influence: Consider the influence of the arts and cultural community on immigration to specific locations. Arts and culture helps to build diversity that mutually supports artistic practice, immigrant inclusion, neighborhood development, tolerance, and broad-mindedness.

Historical influence: Embrace your history and, in particular, those contexts driven from authentic and unique contributions to local and regional evolution. Consider aspects of history, culture, immigration, industry, and more. Be open-minded to embrace artists' interpretation of recent-and-emerging realities to portray a well-rounded story with both historical and present-day context. Be proud of your history, but don't get stuck there as you may miss emerging, unique, and contemporary assets that identify and re-brand your community, potentially adding to its vibrancy and attractiveness.

Artistic Driver #6: Economics

Not by coincidence, I present economics as the last artistic driver.

Generally, artists are not motivated by money. Rather, they are motivated by their innate need to create. Money is important, of course. We live in a capitalist society and money is part of that equation. However, there seems to be an imbalance of revenue-generating initiatives within government and business circles that focus on return on investment, economic development, and creative industries as opposed to focusing on initiatives that *invest in creative content* and *reinvest in those who initiate creative content.* These conversations and policy initiatives suggest a lack of knowledge and understanding of the true value of the arts on the part of some creative industry and business benefactors; the truth is, this should be of critical interest to both.

In the larger creative economy supply chain, creative industry stakeholders benefit monetarily from creative content distributed within the industry segment of the arts ecosystem. There is little evidence these benefactors reinvest a portion of revenues into a fund or similar depository that directly supports creative artistic producers (artists, arts organizations), the bedrock upon which their success is built. Core cultural producers (artists) who germinate the creative content often strive to survive on menial compensation for their work.

The 'starving artist' stereotype helps no one. Compensation to artists needs to better align with their inherent value and impact on society. As economies and societies evolve, so too must our respect for core artistic producers, without whom our world would be sadly diminished.

Our capitalist economy is built on a system that all sectors are beholden to, one way or another. The capitalist system is one in which corporations hold tight to shareholder primacy, that is, they focus on shareholders' needs as their primary concern. What I am alluding to when I speak of reinvesting in those who initiate creative content is building wealth equity into our capitalist economy for the benefit of many, not a few. Taking this idea one step further, initiatives can be adapted by individual corporations and sectors through corporate social responsibility programs. A better approach, through a long-term (and seismic) shift in systems, would redirect wealth equity via "stakeholder capitalism, a system that shares the spoils of victory with those who make it possible"[xxxiii].

This might be the topic for another book, but for now I want to introduce the model to you, my readers. It is a high-level concept that interlocks with the underlying focus of this book as related to partnerships and holistic community development; the concept aligns with my primary focus on the arts sector and artists as *those who make all else within the ecosystem possible.* How does economics directly affect artists?

It is well known that most artists exist within the middle-to-low income bracket of society. Besides what I have outlined above, I speak more about this in Chapter 9, *Let's Get Social.* I want to emphasize here that valuing artists and their work MUST be repositioned in society's consciousness as innate, beyond 'entertainment' and 'nice to have' perceptions and artists MUST be better paid for their work. How we (as a society and a sector) redefine and reconstruct compensation and business models that value not only artists but also their ability to thrive will determine the long-term impacts of artistic creativity in our local communities and global societies.

Beyond concerns about value for work, artists have come under additional pressure to self-manage their careers including marketing themselves, building and maintaining their public profile, selling their product, and adapting technology to creatively present their artworks. Where is the time and head space to create? An increasing number of amateur and professional artists vie for the public's attention, many with access to digital tools to create and distribute work; some artists do not have reliable internet connectivity, rendering them at a disadvantage. The online marketplace is sizable, yet the internet highway is crowded, increasing the challenge to be heard and seen amongst high volumes of competing content.

Technological industry giants solicit subscription dollars in return for streaming artistic content, while retaining a significant percentage of money for themselves. Consider a Facebook post by Canadian music artist Danny Michel on November 20, 2018, where he claimed that streaming revenue for an artist is "$0.003 per play on Spotify."[xxxiv] One of his songs "has been in the TOP 20 charts [of Canadian Broadcasting Corporation *Radio 2* and *Radio 3*] for ten weeks, climbing to #3. In 2018, that equals $44.99 in sales." He also stated, "up to 24 percent of musical professionals indicated they were considering leaving the industry," taken from a study by the

Unison Benevolent Fund, an organization that "is here to help professional music makers in times of hardship, illness, or economic difficulties."[xxxv]

And what about distribution frameworks for those artists whose artistic matter is delivered on a stable medium (*analog*) as opposed to an unstable medium (*digital*)? If distribution is linked to revenues and traditional networks, and these are being eroded, how does an artist make money? And without money, how can an artist continue to create? Are professional artists currently under-rated more than ever? Has their intrinsic value been lost? And, if so, to what?

Artists seek, buy, and obtain their raw materials and tools (paint, guitars, electronic equipment, weaving looms, pottery wheels and clay, fabric, canvas, frames, computers, paper, and so on) to produce their artwork. This material costs money. Artists are entrepreneurs; they sell their work. However, many have developed their business and marketing skills through trial and error or workshops and, although intelligent, many artists struggle in these areas. Cooperative entrepreneurial clusters are a feasible solution that provide a platform for sales, promotion, and public engagement (see the *Quidi Vidi* case study at the end of this chapter).

Artists support consumerism when purchasing their own supplies and through the purchase of other artworks. It is common practice for artists to reinvest their revenues to develop new creative works or to purchase others' artwork.

Keeping their production costs low and establishing additional revenue sources are crucial to survival as an artist. Other measures include:

- Affordable housing costs.
- Bulk purchases (either singularly or within a group of artists).
- Finding alternative work, full-time or part-time (ideally associated with their primary career as an artist; this is possible but rare).
- Seeking contracts, new clients, and creative consulting through retail, event, and partnership opportunities, perhaps working through arts councils or other intermediaries.
- Advocating to municipalities to reduce overall tax and rental fees or adjust zoning bylaws. This measure supports long-term activity of the sector, benefiting the municipality overall.

How do other arts ecosystem stakeholders economically support or benefit from the presence of artists in their community? Many impacts are well known but let me elaborate.

Arts Organizations

Revenues: In Canada, many arts organizations access government funding, sourced revenues, and programming revenues (e.g., ticket sales, sponsorship, or funding campaign) to operate. Operational funding is often tied to entities with national scope and is limited but is increasingly accessible to more contemporary arts sector initiatives. Arts organizations, generally, present creative works developed through artistic disciplines or serve arts sector memberships.

Skills development: Arts organizations offer artists skills and creative development opportunities; such programs may include artist-in-residence programs, discipline-specific training, retreats, and other forms of individual or group skills-based training. Results lead to new creative artworks which both contribute to authenticity of place and intersect with cross-sectoral levers for economic and arts sector development.

Intermediaries: Arts organizations gather and distribute funds to artists through their programs, supporting cross-pollination or sole creative development. Some opportunities build local and national networks for artists to utilize in advancing their work.

Knowledge / Connectivity: Working together and in consultation with artists and other primary arts ecosystem stakeholders, arts organizations share knowledge of available cultural resources. Arts organizations sit at the hub and are a primary interdisciplinary and cross-sectoral connector that supports both economic and creative activity.

Heritage and Museums

Patrons: Organizations can cross-pollinate their patrons from those who are interested in, attend, or explore arts and cultural interests elsewhere. For example, work with partners to develop a multi-access pass with only one payment required by the patron to attend various types of arts, heritage, and museum programming.

Alternate revenue streams: Be creative. Build unconventional partnerships that infuse curiosity into products and venues. Consider displaying local artwork for sale by commission: champion others' work. Imperatively, know your spending limits/budgets and stay within them.

Leverage your assets: Build a story around your place in the community that reflects historical and present-day realities. Use this story to attract locals as much as tourists, incorporating hidden or uncommon facts, celebrating local patrons and their contributions, and highlighting physical or intangible infrastructure. Consider profiling present-day (or recent-day) people linked to historical contexts. Dig to find stories or shifts over the years not currently promoted or are lesser-known.

Residents

Residents support artists and/or benefit from their presence in their community economically when they:

- Purchase tickets to performances, film screenings, and other events.
- Volunteer in many capacities within arts organizations, festivals, or events.
- Spend money on meals, drinks, or transportation associated with either volunteer or social activities when participating in arts and cultural interests.

- Purchase tangible or intangible artist-inspired and creative artworks.
- Support sponsorship of art-based events and activities through their workplace.
- Donate to creative projects through online funding campaigns.
- Voluntarily generate word-of-mouth or social media promotion that drives audiences to events and activities who then spend money there.

Municipalities

Tax Incentives: Taxes are both collected and subsidized by municipalities to increase the presence of creative industries, business and building owners, housing, artist studios, retailers, galleries, and other resources and supports for artists.

Sponsorship: Municipalities provide long-term support for events/programs that generate economic spin-offs or increase visitation to the municipality, commonly with a focus on specific outcomes. Another form of sponsorship includes acting as a funding partner to assist an arts organization in accessing funding with another level of government.

Integrate artworks: Municipalities act as leaders in promoting the visibility of local artwork (and the artists) by integrating artists and their artwork into operations. They act as a champion for the arts, encouraging local businesses and organizations to do the same.

Community support: A company's corporate social responsibility program can focus on the arts sector to invest in community sustainability and artistic creativity. Businesses championing these principles engage their staff to complement their efforts through corporate program engagement and support the arts sector through their own initiative.

Clients: Invite business with artists by way of creative partnerships and promotions that address needs of artists and arts organizations and stimulate general interest in art.

Labour: Consider hiring artists either in their primary creative scope of work or as contract staff to support business operations. Utilize a pool of artists with various skillsets to support your short-term business and labour needs.

Leadership: Servant leadership is a transformational management practice that empowers and values staff through their contributions to operations, open communication, valued inputs, and the ability to work (somewhat) autonomously with overall leadership steering the ship. Under this leadership, an organizational culture exhibits positive relations, staff retention is high, and revenues generally reflect the optimism of staff. Integrate this management practice by inviting staff input that taps into their interests and knowledge when developing corporate social responsibility programs, targeting new ways to support the local arts sector.

Technology: Technology companies are the new platform or intermediary for artworks and its distribution (in some cases).

The creative economy and creative industries increasingly rely on technology as a development and delivery tool. Scalable technology platforms that direct (or redirect) higher revenues to artists and arts organizations is both a significant gap and a significant opportunity to reinvest in the grass-roots level of the arts and cultural sector.

Government

Taxes: Consider new ways to reflect artists' flexible and inconsistent income cycles, including reporting and payment schedules. Overhaul tax policies and legislation that prevent or limit fund-matching opportunities to incentivize businesses, foundations, and other philanthropic sources, thereby opening the door to new social enterprise investment resources for artists and arts sector intermediaries not currently available.

Reinvestment / Commissions: Collaborate and consult with the arts sector to develop new reinvestment methods that support the sector. Consider creative industry operational revenues or other scalable creative economy entities that benefit from but do not currently reinvest in artistic, creative, and content development phases of the arts ecosystem. Redirect these and other corporate proceeds as direct investment dollars that better compensate core artistic creators (artists). Review copyright legislation and royalty payment guidelines to better value, acknowledge, and compensate artists for their IP and its ongoing use.

Tourism and culture departments: Develop cross-sectoral alliances that partner with arts sector service organizations, arts sector leaders, tourism agencies, venues, and other stakeholders to build mutually beneficial programming and marketing that equitably supports all stakeholders.

Immigration: Appreciate how immigrant retention is linked to rooted community integration. The arts sector offers programming that draws immigrants through interactive, participatory, and inclusionary forces. Artists, arts organizations, and their associated networks offer many resources on which to build a valuable and effective partner—recognizing the arts are one gateway to retain newcomers.

Evidence-based planning: Work with members at (or with connections to) the grass roots of the arts sector when developing short- and long-term initiatives that impact arts sector stakeholders. Consider the impact of such initiatives on the arts sector within all aspects of planning tied to economic growth, social well-being, technology, environmental issues, and subsequent outcomes affecting other sectors tied to artistic creation (e.g., tourism, restaurants, hotels, healthcare, and others).

Artistic Driver #7: Education (Post-secondary)

The artistic driver *Education* emerged only marginally in my research compared with other primary drivers of the arts ecosystem. Post-secondary educational institutions influence (to some degree) where an artist lives. These factors apply to all ecosystem stakeholders to varying degrees, so I list the intersecting benefits within this summary.

Educational institutions affect a community and, by association, the artists who live there. The impacts are both direct and indirect.

Presence: Post-secondary educational institutions infuse a community with academic research and knowledge that generates broad-minded, creative thinkers. Cultural influences of inbound professors and student populations seep into a community's local fabric.

Continual development of artistic practices raises artists' professional development and expertise. Often, access to local professional development opportunities is the most feasible option. Artist-in-residence programs linking to community development often exhibit highly successful outcomes.[xxxvi] (See the Case Study *Open House* at the end of Chapter 6.)

Diversity: Cultural and intellectual diversity aligns with academic institutions, expanding the potential for development and growth. Visual diversity, as in a population where varied cultures of origin are present, exhibits and attracts inclusionary forces.

Intellectual stimulation from direct or indirect educational influence supports an artistic practice through resources and opportunities for research and knowledge building, where an idea can develop into a creative artwork.

Creativity and arts training in an educational milieu influence problem-solving, tolerance, team building, and independent thinking, particularly in children engaged in artistic disciplines during their youth. Subsequently, these important traits are highly valued in many career professions.

Teamwork: Many arts disciplines bring together multiple people or contributors (for example, theatre, musical bands, dance troupes, and other works that require a diverse team). Working together requires critical thinking and resulting solutions that reflect teamwork skills. These are transferable life skills that are highly valued in many career professions.

- *Creative works* describes an artist's creative output, regardless of their chosen discipline. The conditions that support artistic output vary, including where an artist lives, their access to resources, available arts sector infrastructure, audiences, and many other factors.

- Artists often seek a place to live that inspires their creativity and perhaps offers a muse. The stimulation they seek can be associated with environmental beauty and available resources that influence or support their work. Rural and small urban areas offer an affordable cost of living and fewer barriers to entry.

- Large urban areas offer additional income opportunity for artists, such as teaching opportunities, gig-economy contract work and options to work in non-artistic professions that may correlate with their creative abilities.

- Arts organizations act as primary access points for non-arts-centric stakeholders to engage and partner with the arts sector and its creative riches. Arts leaders are positioned like the hub of a wheel, the point of receiving and sharing information for others' benefit, across sectors and networks.

- Primary linkage to the arts ecosystem is through owners and staff at business and arts service organizations and entities that offer support to arts entrepreneurs such as arts incubators and accelerators.

- When considering arts sector planning, a shared vision invites arts sector stakeholders to participate in alliance discussions. Stakeholders investigate opportunities for mutually-beneficial multi-sector partnerships, expanding visions and generating a web of support that extends to ecosystem stakeholders.

- Rural communities that seek to value the arts sector beyond economic generation are well positioned to benefit from next generation arts sector development. Municipalities recognize the importance of *liveable cities* by building social equity and inclusion through community-based, socially-engaged neighbourhoods that include a vibrant arts ecology.

- Understand the value of cultural districts with a cautious eye to development. Some forms of urban development, such as gentrification, can force artists to abandon vibrant neighbourhoods where their creativity influences attraction of others. Gentrification leads to increased rental costs for studios and living accommodations, beyond what artists can afford, forcing them out of the district they created.

- Compensation to artists needs to better align with their inherent value and impact on society. As economies and societies evolve, so too must our respect for the creative producers, without whom our world would be sadly diminished.

- The capitalist system is such that corporations hold tight to shareholder primacy, focusing on shareholders' needs as their primary concern. A more holistic system would redirect wealth equity via *stakeholder capitalism*, a system that shares the spoils of victory with those who make it possible—in this case, artists.

- Beyond concerns about value for work, many artists are under pressure to self-manage their careers: marketing themselves, building and maintaining their public profile; sales (online and in-person), and adapting to technology platforms. Where is the time and space to create?

- Technology is a new tool and might be considered an intermediary for artwork creation and distribution. Scalable technology platforms offer a significant opportunity for industry to reinvest dollars back into the grass roots to encourage ongoing creative success.

- Individuals or businesses holding technology expertise should consider sharing their skills with arts organizations or artists through resource-sharing partnerships or other means that build win-win prospects.

- Educational institutions have both direct and indirect impacts on artists, the community in which they live, and potential creative outcomes through creative development, diversity, and intellectual stimulation.

Case Study: Quidi Vidi Plantation, Newfoundland, Canada

RE: CROSS-SECTORAL PARTNERSHIPS: ARTS EDUCATION, ENTREPRENEURS, MUNICIPALITY, TOURISM

When undertaking research for an artisan cooperative, I considered the feasibility for growth in this artistic discipline within the (micro) client organization and on a (macro) regional/provincial level. I visited *The Quidi Vidi Plantation* in the eastern region of the City of St. John's, Newfoundland (located approximately one mile from the City's downtown core) to inform my work.

A once-active building in the fishing village was in disrepair by the 1990s. It held historical significance to the community and at the same time the local artisan (craft arts) community recognized their need for studio space. The Quidi Vidi Development Plan (2003) set the wheels in motion to transform the building into a multi-functional space for events, an artisan incubator, and a tourist information center. The primary operational partners were the City of St. John's, the Craft Council of Newfoundland and Labrador, and the College of the North Atlantic's *Textiles: Craft Apparel and Design* program. Funding partners included federal/provincial/municipal levels of government and business-focused funding sources.

The project provides much-needed studio space for artisans while fostering business for emerging artists. Students apply for residency in the space. Residency gives students a platform to launch into the business world, a subsidized studio space, face-to-face access to customer sales (the location is a growing tourism and event destination), opportunities to build relationships with other occupants, and ongoing support of notable operational partners. This incubator framework supports artisans in building their business and a sustainable career while contributing to overall community economic growth.

This project model addressed the objectives and goals of multiple partners:

- The City of St. John's, looking for economic growth via increased business opportunities and willing to invest, leveraged support from other beneficiaries and financial partners.
- The municipality sought to retain an important feature of its heritage, dovetailing to further develop a tourism destination.
- The Craft Council sought space to enhance individual artisan's skills and capacity to develop a viable career while boosting the number of practising artisans in the region.
- A demand for increased studio space by artisans was addressed.
- The College wanted to extend their programs that gave graduating artisans a greater chance of financial and career success.

The key person in this development was the executive director of the Craft Council of Newfoundland and Labrador. She was the common thread that tied all partners and elements of the project together. She facilitated conversations among city, scholastic and artisan partners; guided development of the project; and provided continuity between the college, the students, and the incubator space at the Plantation. Overall, she was the ongoing orchestrator of the project's success.

It often takes one person who brings continuity and leadership to optimize project facilitation. In succession planning, transferring the thread of responsibility to another person can be tricky and requires significant planning, knowledge transfer, and communication before, during and after the transition period to ensure that significant knowledge and relationships are not lost.

8

Your Unique Assets

At this point, you should have a good understanding of the arts ecosystem. Now we will build a roadmap to partnerships based on your local community. The stakeholders outlined within the ecosystem framework will help to inform potential relationships, alignments, and possibilities as we think about assets at the local level. Many assets double as resources, meaning something or someone you can access and hope to utilize, and who will support your objectives.

The good news is you only have to do this exercise once. Tweaking the original list is an ongoing but not arduous task to manage. The bad news is, well, nothing. You are building a timeless tool that supports your organization or your artistic practice. Implementing these suggestions provides a hands-on approach to explore new opportunities. How creative you get is up to you.

When you think of assets, what comes to mind? It depends on the context.

Within Your Organization

Are you thinking within an organizational context? If yes, assets might include:

- human resources (paid and volunteer)

- physical structure(s) or site-specific work areas (auditorium, studios, library, office space, or other built environments)
- specific skillsets available through staff, board, or volunteers
- technology hardware and software
- inventories (office/art supplies, costumes, historical files, and other resources)
- programming (content, audiences, creators)

And the list goes on.

Does your organization have unique assets in your local community? How and why are these assets unique?

If you refer to the *Key Findings* in Chapter 5, you will remember it is important to include the *unique* assets rooted in your community or organization. These assets may be well known and used in publicity formats, or perhaps they have yet to be recognized as assets.

Historical references, former traditions, and stories are sometimes buried in the past for any number of reasons. As our society changes, historical facts once deemed unspeakable or simply not considered relevant might hold significant interest in present-day contexts. Perhaps a local practice or everyday occurrence has been overlooked as a noteworthy asset. Should you be the first to highlight an important fact, relationship, or historic event during this mapping exercise, you might gain a distinctive competitive advantage to leverage this knowledge as unique to your organization or community.

External Cultural Assets

Mapping cultural assets develops a pool of resources. Here, I summarize arts and cultural sector references to guide you:[xxxvii]

- Spaces and Facilities (design studios, theatres, museums, libraries, parks, digital media studios, and others)
- Intangible Assets (stories, place names, oral traditions, fictional characters, and ceremonies)
- Cultural Heritage (buildings, cemeteries, heritage districts, historic sites, and archaeological sites)
- Nature Heritage (parks, farms, orchards, botanical gardens, zoos, conservation authorities, and landscape architects)
- Festivals and Events (film, multicultural, performance, gallery/studio tours, public art tours, cultural and heritage tours, and so many more)
- Creative / Cultural Industries (commercial galleries, publishers, film/video/sound recording studios, pottery studios, theatre companies, photography, radio and television, gaming/animation companies, hi-tech firms, and others)
- Community Cultural Organizations (community-based arts, historical and genealogical societies, Indigenous cultures, multicultural organizations, and others)

Here are a few more considerations:

- *Who* might be considered among your community's *local cultural assets* that you can leverage?

o   Noteworthy people (deceased or alive), personalities, fictional characters. These too can be considered assets when associated with a specific place. For example, *Anne of Green Gables* is an iconic and highly visible tourist attraction in Prince Edward Island but, in reality, is a fictional character created by author Lucy Maud Montgomery. This character has spawned a tourism industry and many spin-off businesses such as overnight accommodations, branded chocolates, signature 'straw hat and braids' memorabilia, a golf course, a musical theatre production (50+ year consecutive run), a television show, numerous movies, and much more.

- *Where* are these and other assets located?

  o   Think about proximity to other compatible and comparable assets. Perhaps you identify an existing cluster of attractions or a developing cultural district. Consider geographic connection, creative association, a specific topic, or other cross-cutting themes when investigating potential linkage. For example, an arts school in a neighbouring community that you invite to provide classes for local artists; or you present programming in their community.

Community Assets

How should you consider assets within a larger local community ecosystem context? From this perspective assets might include:

- training programs and spaces
- presentation venues
- galleries, studios, libraries, and creative/community hubs
- the proximity/size of your geographic location, with the associated advantages and disadvantages
- businesses and organizations that directly benefit from your work
- businesses and organizations who you gain knowledge and support from, either paid or in lieu
- chambers of commerce
- community organizations, youth groups
- local suppliers to your organization (printing, marketing collateral, web/technology, food, hardware)

And the list goes on.

You are expanding your viable asset base, developing a broader list of community assets outside arts sector or traditional partnership contexts than were outlined previously. Let me stress this point. The list of assets you are developing is important because they exist *in YOUR local community*.

Know which businesses or assets are rooted in your community because local businesses carry significant importance in this process. Why? Rooted businesses are less likely to leave your neighborhood unexpectedly. Long-term relationships co-exist well with organizations deeply-rooted in your community.

Large retail chain businesses are not considered rooted in a community when decision making occurs at corporate offices located elsewhere. But, there are exceptions as franchises are run locally. These businesses have a positive impact on small communities, so a good guideline is to consider them if you have local access to them. Why? They may seek an opportunity to connect locally in a meaningful way if that is a strong value within their head office. Your organization may be a gateway for them.

Now that you have hundreds of contacts and ideas swirling in your head, I suggest you write them down. Start with arts organizations and suppliers with whom you work. These should come easily to you. Semi-organize your list as you go, grouping into three categories: organizational assets, external cultural assets, and community assets.

Your list will continue to expand as you drill down into organizations or businesses who would be a good fit with your organization. Determining factors include shared values, shared networks, and value propositions, meaning what you (or they) bring to a partnership that increases value to your (and their) audiences (customers). Think with unlimited possibility what assets (yours and theirs) would make a unique, mutually-beneficial partnership.

Developing and Organizing Your Priorities

The list of people, organizations, businesses and internal assets you develop combines to create a foundational list of organizational, cultural and community assets; this list guides how and with whom you develop unique and creative partnerships. You have begun to organize your thoughts into separate headings to capture:

1. Your organization's assets (internal, organizational,
    networks, unique, and so on). You previously outlined
    these assets.

2. Cultural assets (local, hubs, historical, architectural,
    language, Indigenous, artistic, unique, ethnic, public art,
    traditions, events and more).

3. Community assets (hubs, historical, architectural,
    language, Indigenous, artistic, ethnic, unique, events,
    and others). This is a list you previously started to
    compile, perhaps finished?

Strategic Targets, Objectives, Priorities

Before selecting who from your list might make a good partner,
first consider your organization's strategic targets and
objectives. Why? If you clearly understand what your
organization wants to achieve you can more easily determine
the resources required to deliver on these objectives. This step
avoids eagerly going off in multiple directions. Stay focused on
current objectives and targets. You can flex your creative
muscles during the implementation phase. If your organization
has a strategic plan already in place, your strategic targets and
objectives are confirmed.

If you do not have a strategic plan in place, not to worry. You or
your Board of Directors have probably outlined priorities for the
current year in broad terms with SMART (specific, measurable,
achievable, realistic, timely) goals.

If you do not have a list of priorities outlined in a SMART format, you should complete this task, in cooperation with your board before moving forward. Reflect on plans for your current year of operation; optimally, consider future operations within a three- to five-year period.

Once you have your goals and objectives outlined, determine:

- Which are priority items?
- Are any goals/objectives interlinked? (Does the success of one depend on the development or completion of something else first?)
- What are notable annual cycles within your operation? (It is helpful to write these out within an annual or monthly calendar.)
- Do annual cycles affect your ability to develop and implement new partnerships? How?

Thinking through these items will help you develop a mix of targets and objectives that range from easily obtained wins for priority items and achievement of long-term goals. When you cross-reference required resources to achieve each objective, you are moving closer in determining potential partners.

You are sizing up your organization's needs, gaps, and wants while sourcing partnership options to reach your operational goals. Here are questions to help determine which priority items you should tackle:

- What are your priority goals (broad) and objectives (specific)? You outlined these under SMART goals.
- What resources do you require to achieve these goals?

- What gaps or barriers exist to acquire necessary or beneficial resources and/or partnerships (for example, funding, grant deadlines, marketing resources, vacation periods, technology, or other limiting factors).
  - Search potential partners' websites and become knowledgeable about present support for community initiatives. This will provide insight about their company values, areas of interest, corporate social responsibility focus, and corporate expertise to then determine potential linkages that fit with your organization's goals and resource gaps.
  - Who or what is your competition?
  - It is beneficial for this competitor to become a partner?
  - If yes, how do you position this to them as an opportunity?
  - Outline *why you want to collaborate with them* (make them feel special).
  - Outline *how* a partnership benefits *them* (short-term and long-term), depending on your/their goal(s).
  - Be prepared to share your short and long-term goals. Be positive and highlight your credibility (past successes and growth indicators).
  - Share other measures you are taking to meet your organizational and programming goals.
  - Consider multi-partnership collaborations. Alliances of three-or-more partners are quite attractive as they lessen risk and increase value for each partner.

Building Partnerships That Support Strategic Targets and Objectives

Now you are ready to match up potential resources, partners, and assets (internal and external). You are creating a list of people and organizations you want to work with who will equally benefit from working with you and your organization.

An important aspect of partnerships is *effective relationships*. Focus on building relationships through authentic and genuine curiosity for other people. Understand *their* likes, *their* wants, *their* values, and *their* goals. You already know why you are interested in partnering with them and you know your wants, values, and goals, but they may know little to nothing about you. They are at a disadvantage, so you want to position a new relationship as something that will benefit *them.* If you do, you will have their attention.

Be prepared to introduce how your organization will also benefit from your proposed partnership. Transparency is vitally important.

Remember, your primary objective in finding partners is to enable *you* to reach the goals *you previously outlined.* You are seeking resources or assets that support your efforts. These resources are your potential partners with whom you want to reciprocate their contribution(s) with your unique assets that have value for them.

At this point, you have a list of your organization's priority objectives and a broad list of local assets. Now you want to identify who from your personal and professional contacts intersect with these assets and organizations.

Partnerships Values

To establish a **primary partnership list**, match your preferred external assets (organizations) and resources to your priority objective list. When completed, align your personal contacts with the organizations or businesses listed. You may be surprised how many companies you have established connections with. This means you are not starting from ground zero to build a relationship, which is a real benefit as networking and building relationships takes time.

When working through these steps, consider each organization's *values* and whether these values align with those of your organization. If you are unsure, make a note to do some further research on this organization or business. *If values do not align, recognize this early and redirect your energy elsewhere.* Entering into a partnership based on differing values can lead to unmet expectations and frustrating, potentially damaging, outcomes for either partner.

Here are a few more questions to consider as you refine your list of potential partners. These questions focus on how a partner benefits your organization.

- How, specifically, do these organizations bridge a gap to your goals?

- Is the resource/asset renewable, meaning can it be used multiple times? (Ideally, yes. You want to leverage long-term relationships and benefits.)
- Does the resource/asset build capacity in your organization?
- Would a partnership positively enhance your organization's public profile?
- Is the potential partner someone you would enjoy working with?
- Are a partner's expectations achievable and sustainable for your organization?

If you discover limited opportunities, unrealistic expectations, or limited areas of common interest, move on to the next name on your list. ***Concentrate on working with organizations that see the value of your work and offer benefits to the relationship.*** You are determining a fit for an intended, long-term partnership. You want to recognize suitability factors from the start and deepen the partnership over time. True partnerships offer the option of building new programs and initiatives, together.

The strongest partnerships are built upon relationships where:

- Both parties have a vested interest. (The reasons for interest may vary. That is OK.)
- The partners mutually understand and support each other's stated objectives.
- Each partner believes in the work, values, goals, objectives, and potential outcomes of the other.

- Partners agree upon targets to assess and measure the impacts for each partner, the community, and other stated objectives.
- Outcomes meet *ALL* partners' expectations, focusing on how everybody wins.

Unique and Relevant Benefits

As you go through this process, consider what unique and relevant benefits you can offer potential partners. Reference your internal asset list. Identify what you can offer that benefits *them*: their business goals, their philanthropic agenda (corporate social responsibility program), or broader community goals.

If you are not sure what these are, you have to do some research. Your personal contact at the company is one way to learn more; conducting an internet search or investigating their website are other methods. If your discoveries leave questions, inquire directly with the organization for clarification. You will be well-informed and well-positioned to eventually introduce yourself. A soft introduction might occur through online business platforms like LinkedIn or at a Chamber or community mixer. Connect and use the opportunity to introduce yourself, briefly. You might be surprised by the other person's interest or curiosity regarding your work. After all, you work in a highly creative (and, to some, mysterious) sector.

Remember: an inquiry or an introduction is not a pitch! If you approach it as such you may miss an opportunity for a strong, targeted approach later on. At this point, you are in a period of discovery. You are seeking mutual areas of interest or perhaps an initiative that entices a potential partner. Finding this strengthens your value during an eventual pitch.

When the time does come to pitch an idea or partnership, you want to be armed with many realistic, potential benefits that interest your partner. The information noted below helps to build a list tailored to the partner:

- What are exclusive, tailored benefits *(be creative here)* you can provide for each potential partner? Think both short-term and long-term, while realizing a trial period will be expected.
- Provide *unique* benefits that address opportunity from the partner's perspective.
- Did you consider an anniversary or new initiative (of theirs) that position these benefits within a unique or limited window of opportunity?

Creative Benefits

Here are a few examples of *thinking outside the box* when identifying creative benefits:

- If you are a venue, can you offer free space for a potential partner to hold meetings, receptions, or an annual celebration?
- Do you have access to costumes that you can rent at a reduced partner rate?
- Can you offer reduced rental space fees?
- Perhaps you eliminate additional fees on a regular facility rental (for example, staff costs are included).

- You can offer free subscription(s) or free tickets to support your partner's goal in wooing clients. (This is a perk the other partner can leverage to appeal to *their* clients.)
- Can you offer a free workshop for your partner's staff (such as a dance class, a writing workshop, a closed rehearsal) as a perk?
- Consider what you can leverage through your membership if you are an arts service organization. This benefit doubles as an opportunity to expose non-arts patrons to your facility, an artistic discipline, or some aspect of the arts sector while breaking down self-imposed barriers of exclusion.
- Offer private or exclusive benefits such as tours, opportunities to present or speak (for a partner representative) at your events (opening nights, media events, program launches, or other artistic activities), newsletter contributions, and other means to acknowledge their role as a partner.
- Develop unique benefits that inspire and include your partner's staff as a component of their corporate social responsibility program. Inquire what your partner and/or their staff would appreciate by including them in the process, then you are assured what you offer is of value to the recipients. Collaborative design of partnership benefits deepens relationships on multiple levels: between partners and staff at both organizations and through communication channels to build trust and reciprocity.

Your Pitch

The more unique you are, the more memorable you will be. Keep this in mind for your presentations and your pitches.

Below are a few creative examples to consider when developing a unique approach for your pitch:

- If you have publications showing the history of your organization, distribute one or more copies when you give your presentation.
- If your organization offers a unique product sourced through another partner (a special product at your bar, like specialized chocolate or handmade products), highlight this partnership in your presentation by offering a sample of the product. This shows a potential partner that 1) you have other partners, 2) you value these partners, and 3) you are savvy about cross-marketing unique offerings obtained through partnerships. The underlying message is that you may do the same for them.
- Include a live presentation with actors/singers, such as a short excerpt from a production at your venue. Consider the context of your audience, where you are presenting, whether the presentation is live or via digital methods, and the scope of your potential partnership.
- Bring props, as appropriate, that support your presentation.
- Include a short, compelling, professional, digital presentation that captures successful programs and unique assets in your organization.

- Include testimonials from youth, long-time supporters, sponsors, and other partners' staff to your pitch. Don't include them 'just because.' Be sure they support your pitch.
- Offer free tickets—two for each person listening to your presentation—inviting them to a regular or special event in the near future, one that will take place within two to four weeks.
- Ideally, highlight one or more unique opportunities for this potential partner. Present an offer they will find hard to resist, while impressing upon them you have done your research (without stating this directly).
- Emphasize your organization's assets. Be creative...you play and work in the creative sector!

Keep it simple but make an impression. You will invite curiosity while welcoming non-arts-centric arts ecosystem stakeholders to take a seat at the arts table.

Relationship Building

Next, we turn to the concept of *relationship marketing*. This is a simple long-term approach that overlays partnerships and involves positive relationship building. The intent is to take a person from awareness of your product or institution to an advocacy role. It takes time, trust, and many positive interactions along the way.

Many people are familiar with a transactional relationship: an exchange of time or money for something in return. When searching for such transactions, traditional marketing tactics and methods are often applied, such as advertising, media applications (interviews, press releases, social media, and so on), promotional materials, and more. The opportunity to move beyond transactional exchanges arises when *you* invest in developing a deeper relationship.

So how do you do this?

1. Be aware of the opportunity.
2. Make a conscious decision to work in this manner.
3. Develop your short- and long-term strategic objectives with this concept in mind.
4. Communicate with your staff and board *why* you are taking this approach.
5. Be willing to play the long game.

Communication

Implementing the concept of relationship building relies on communication. Overall, communication is a key component in building trust, understanding, and relationships. The most intimidating step for many can be initiating contact for the first time. Although armed with your research, you may feel outside your comfort zone when meeting new people. Prepare before a meeting or phone call with a list of items to discuss; practising your pitch in advance also helps to reduce your anxiety and build your confidence.

Brainstorm how to best reach your intended audience. Use multi-pronged approaches. Ensure your messaging is conveyed through multiple sources with an air of welcome and genuine invitation. It is important to realize self-imposed barriers are a reality to many who do not participate in the arts. Find creative ways to not only reach but also connect with those who do not currently engage.

Always have a next step to offer partners for engagement such as an opportunity for volunteers, patrons, sponsors, or partners to broaden their contribution, if desired. You gauge what is mutually beneficial over time and by getting to know your supporters, personally. This takes time.

Be prepared to communicate with your partners (and supporters) regularly. Any effort you make in this area builds credibility and deepens the relationship. Commit to providing supporters with interim updates on new initiatives, positive growth, and incremental success stories directly related to their support. Provide opportunity for interactive communication such as a town hall or webinar event. Your unsolicited outreach goes a long way to build value and appreciation among your supporters. This is in addition to regularly scheduled meetings, annual subscription purchases, or annual donor campaigns.

Every external public speaking engagement and communication opportunity offers a platform to invite arts ecosystem stakeholders to your organization. Doing this often, in a genuine and meaningful way, builds inclusion. Through backstage tours or similar initiatives, you 'lift the veil' on the mystique of the arts for those without innate knowledge about producing in the sector. In other instances, it is first-hand experience that will build trust and enthusiasm.

Genuine, positive interactions with patrons, partners, suppliers, and the media go a long way in generating ongoing, positive, internal, and external relations. We may consciously address sponsorship relationships in this way, but we do not always reflect this approach across all relationships. I find bringing that same intention to all internal and external interactions will generate public support and leapfrog traditional outcomes.

Supporters offer suggestions. Many times, suggestions are viable; often, you need more resources to apply these ideas and/or weave them into your current operations and planning. Sometimes suggestions are unrealistic, perhaps offered with limited knowledge of producing arts events or performances or come from being unfamiliar with managing a not-for-profit operation. The best response is one that educates, tactfully, thereby leading to a fulsome discussion.

One way to acknowledge appreciation for intended support is asking the person suggesting the idea for a solution to your dilemma. You may be surprised with the result. They might offer to contribute more resources. They may know someone who could assist in moving their idea forward. They might join a committee or the board to become more involved. The options are endless.

At this point, the person is willing to bring their knowledge and ideas to your organization, potentially advocating on its behalf. You are in an unenviable position having gained another loyal supporter.

The most important point here is *engagement.* Getting it is the first step, you then realize that *you must manage it,* politely and tactfully with openness and enthusiasm. The better you are at managing these relationships, the more enthusiastic and devoted your supporters will be.

Positive word of mouth is a highly effective tool in development, public relations, and promotional efforts. Lead (and guide) your staff and volunteers to follow your example. When necessary, coach them how to interact with customers, patrons, and each other in this same, consistent, genuine manner. You are inviting participation that builds holistic outcomes.

You are building an organizational culture to which partners are attracted. Curiosity begets attraction.

Leverage what you've got!

Chapter Summary

- Recognize what unique assets you possess in your arts organization.

- Mapping local cultural assets develops a go-to pool of resources for future reference.

- Expand your asset list to include non-arts-centric community organizations.

- Develop or reference a list of strategic priorities, in broad terms with SMART (specific, measurable, achievable, realistic, timely) goals.

- Focus on building relationships through authentic and genuine curiosity about other people to understand *their* likes, *their* wants, *their* values, and *their* goals.

- Ensure that your values align with those of a potential partner.

- Tailor unique and relevant benefits to potential partners.

- Overall, communication is a key component in building trust, understanding, and relationships.

- Genuine, positive interactions with patrons, partners, suppliers, and the media go a long way to generate ongoing, positive internal and external relations.

Case Study: Community Garden, Ottawa Little Theatre, Ontario, Canada

RE: LEVERAGING ASSETS and COMMUNITY PARTNERSHIPS for A STRATEGIC WIN, WIN, WIN!

I managed a theatre in downtown Ottawa that, upon my hire, had untidy raised flower beds to the front and side of the building. I felt the flower beds projected an uninspiring message about the theatre to pedestrians, patrons, and visitors. I wanted to revive the gardens, but the theatre was not in the financial position to spend money on a garden.

I sought a partner and established a shared vision for the garden plots. I reached out through theatre staff and volunteer networks, initially looking for a garden center contact. What surfaced was a local horticultural society contact. We met to investigate project opportunities.

I realized homeless missions were located in my neighborhood close to the theatre. I reached out to one mission, curious about their need for fresh vegetables to feed the homeless, daily. They were delighted to be a benefactor.

All three partners met multiple times and the project emerged. The garden was designed to include specific vegetables and herbs in limited supply at the mission. The design incorporated original and additional flowers and shrubbery for aesthetic purposes.

This successful partnership focused on providing wins for each partner that included:

- A redesigned garden materialized with new soil, repositioned foliage, new foliage, annual vegetables plants, and annual/perennial herb plants.
- The project was paid for by The Horticultural Society, selected as their annual major project that included their volunteer donation of members' time and plants.
- Volunteer resources aggregated from all partners to plant, weed, water, and collect the garden bounty, including garden tools, buckets, and the mission's chefs-in-training candidates.
- The mission's head chef was thrilled to include fresh vegetables and herbs in his menu, adding nutritional and flavorful elements for their clients.

This project leveraged internal and external assets and resources of the theatre and the community while addressing a community need. And although this project had absolutely nothing to do with theatre programming, the project was introduced specifically and strategically to benefit the theatre overall:

- Instill a feeling of pride in staff and volunteers by making a difference in our community, in this case, helping to feed the homeless. This pride expanded to theatre patrons by their association with the theatre.
- Beautify the entrance to the theatre, projecting a feeling of welcome and caring for all.
- Inform the media about our corporate social responsibility project, thereby lifting the profile of the theatre to a wider audience through radio and television coverage of this initiative.

- Show appreciation for our partners and highlight the benefactors through signage erected into the garden.
- Shape positive emotional connection between the theatre and the broader public when promoting the garden story.
- Dovetail the timing and marketing of the garden project with two other initiatives: 1) the theatre's annual subscription campaign, and 2) a capital renovation fundraising campaign, with the purpose to ensure the theatre was 'top of mind' via multiple outreach and promotional strategies.
- Ensure all theatre staff were aware of the partners and benefactors of the garden, should patrons or visitors ask for more information on the project.

Pride in this project extended to all staff and created an emotional connection tied to ownership of the project. As a case in point, the theatre's custodian was in charge of watering the gardens. At one point he informed me 'a well-dressed pedestrian' picked a bean or two when walking by. The custodian addressed the pedestrian saying, "These vegetables are for the homeless, not for the public."

I smiled as I thought, "Community assets, project ownership, and pride are beyond tangible; they are change-makers." Mission accomplished!

9

Let's Get Social!

We humans are social beings. Appreciating *how* and *why* artists impact our society is increasingly important in present-day contexts. Their creative output affects each of us daily. At some level, we see the social value and are engaged in the presence of art, directly or indirectly. However, we do not always recognize or value the impact of art, individually or en masse. That is, until the COVID-19 pandemic reared itself first in China and then across the globe. Country by country, the virus brought much of the world to a standstill in 2020.

Public health officials' plea for physical distancing—a minimum distance of two meters between people—was countered by the human need to connect socially. Our human nature drove many, seemingly instantaneously, to their screens, the internet, video conference platforms, and social media. As we 'sheltered in place' or added hashtags to #StayHome to our social media feeds, abundant amounts of creative content from musicians and actors streamed from living rooms, balconies, and kitchens; theatre and opera archives and museum collections were opened from behind paywalls; and orchestras comforted us with their haunting melodies captured through collective performances and facilitated by digital technology.

Within the first month of a much longer self-isolation period, I noticed stories emerging that focused on the value of the arts and how the arts, regardless of their form, were a welcome anecdote to this period of isolation. The arts brought together strangers from across streets and across the world with appreciation for talents and creativity that amused, entertained, and relieved our fears, if only for a short time. Shared talent was both a relief and a release to the stress and anxiety during this period of time.

I could not help but wonder: Did the arts finally break through a glass ceiling of relative unimportance to some, thrusting and implanting itself into the global consciousness of significant social value? Would there be a lasting, omnipresent value generated during this initial spike through a digital burst of appreciation that would sustain and elevate this sector following months of immobility and crushing losses both during and following this crisis? In fact, given the standstill in global, national, and local economies, I wondered what will survive and emerge from the rubble—and there will be rubble!

Or rather, would the world return to a take-it-or-leave-it disinterest in artists' value and social impact, losing importance following the crisis? What in the value quotient of the arts would be gained or lost overall?

Prior to this global crisis, artistic disciplines were embedded in our daily routines, perhaps without true appreciation: listening to music, watching movies, dancing, streaming content through online platforms, reading books/eBooks, being in the presence of musicians or visual artists at fundraising events or conferences, admiring public art, attending written/visual/music art and cultural festivals, using pottery mugs or wearing hand-crafted jewelry, appreciating architecture that represents societies (current or historical), visiting an art gallery, and so on.

Granted, not all people have a propensity for the arts. Some community members' eyes glaze over, and will continue to do so, when you mention arts. They do not feel affected by or connected to art, socially or otherwise. For those people I wonder:

- Do they read? *Authors are artists.*
- Do they remember a special song that takes them back to their youth or a momentous occasion in their life? *Musicians write songs.*
- Did a movie or theatre production ever awaken an emotion or make them think differently about a given event or topic? *Playwrights, actors, musicians and a host of other artists and technicians contribute to this work.*
- Do they think, "That's cool," when musing about the practical application of visual and contemporary art, whether in a gallery or on the side of a building? *Traditional and contemporary visual artists are creators.*

A significant concern surrounding the influx of artistic content streaming during the COVID-19 pandemic was (presumed) devalued artistic output due to an increased level of free access, meaning active or passive engagement with art at no cost to the consumer. Some argue democratization of the arts is an important component for wider societal inclusion. The appreciative response to share and comment on artistic content during the pandemic is evidence of that. In non-pandemic times, although the intention to expose a greater public to arts is well-placed, is there a negative long-term cost to the artist in presenting perceived 'free art'?

Finding the correct balance is tricky. For example, how do we ensure easily accessible, complimentary art for social pleasure does not diminish perceived or actual value for artists and their expertise? If artists present free product in one context, then does this diminish its value in another? Realizing some venues and organizations have developed programs that rightfully pay artists for their online presentations, all audiences enjoy these concerts without cost.

Is the exorbitant amount of artistic content streamed during the pandemic considered artists' voluntary gift to society (e.g., an artist's give-back response) for their fellow human? Is it valued as such?

As highlighted during the COVID-19 pandemic, the social benefits related to artists' presence in our society go far beyond ticketed events, sponsorship benefits, or entertainment value. Emotional connections are made through art that impact us all, young or old, near or far. The arts are a platform that encourages team building, creative thinking, problem-solving, and friendship. The arts can introduce options and uncertainty to shift the roles and intentions of others. It is hard to measure how personal experience with the arts impacts each of us but this same experience is key to understanding the overall value of the arts among many.[xxxviii]

Children assimilated with the arts learn how to work together, using the sum of all parts to create something bigger than one individual through music, theatre, dance, and other artistic discipline training. They learn to listen, appreciate, make concessions, try new approaches, and take risks. When these soft skills are developed early, they can be applied throughout a person's life. In fact, employers are eager to hire candidates with an arts background given the attributed life skills and experience gained through their arts training.[xxxix]

As noted previously, the arts are also a gateway to relationship building at the community level.

Increasingly, arts programming brings communities together to create, share, learn, and build better communities. This might include a community mural where an artist sketches an outline and invites public participants to add colour. The result is pride in a community project that contributes to expanded networks and inclusionary factors for immigrants, artists, or neighborhood participants who didn't know each other previously. Organizing this project is often arts sector driven by—you guessed it—arts administrators or artists.

Other social values are showcased through larger community development projects such as *Open House*[xl] in York, Alabama. An artist-in-residence project transformed a dilapidated property into a unique, public event space, incorporating assistance from community members, municipal officials, and others who supported the project. (*See the Case Study at the end of Chapter 6.*)

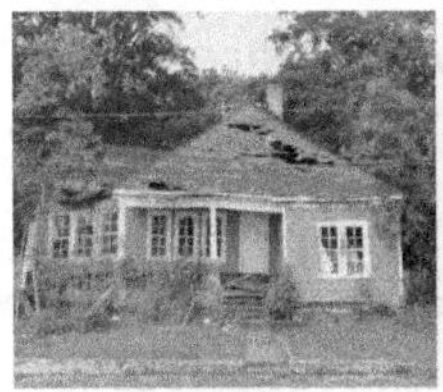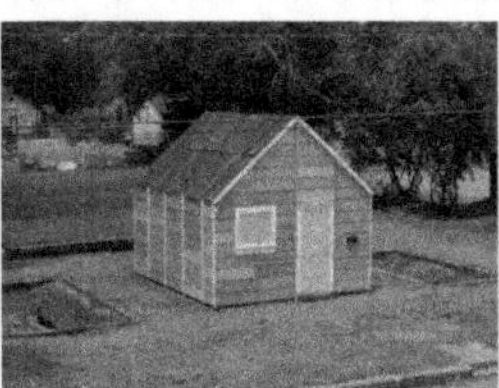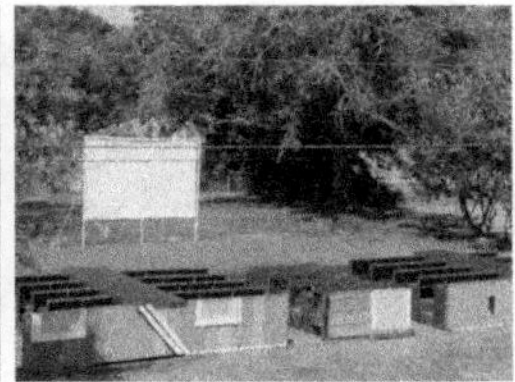

Property photos before and after the "Open House" project in York, Alabama.

In this example, artist Matthew Mazzotta invited residents to participate. He wanted to develop a meaningful project that addressed a *community need* where the community had input from the start. The artist facilitated a project with meaningful long-term, social, inclusionary, and participatory impacts. In the process, the project gained residents' buy-in and ownership for the long-term.

The impacts from this project are multi-faceted:

- *pride* in this new community asset.
- *stewardship* of the property from community members.
- *social benefits* related to play, inclusion, and expression.
- *new relationships and partnerships* among divergent stakeholders.

This list is not exhaustive.

What similar projects has your community undertaken? What projects could your organization lead that could have similar community-building outcomes?

These projects do not easily translate into financial (quantitative) return on investment. However, the ripple effect on social (qualitative) value can be felt in numerous ways. How do you measure smiles and conversation between strangers and new friends? How do you measure 'pride in place'? How do you comparatively measure a rat-infested property now turned into a social gathering place? Through linear comparisons, it is tricky. Based on community and personal well-being, the return on investment is infinite.

A report that I cite throughout this book, *Understanding the Value of Arts and Culture*, addresses the impact of the arts beyond economic and other straight-line measurements, highlighting the overarching value of the arts in human society. It presents research findings from various research projects undertaken for the associated report. Results were published by the Arts and Humanities Research Council (United Kingdom) in 2016. A link to the report is in the reference section of this book and on my website.

The Arts Impact Everyone, Building Value—Daily!

On a personal level, what creative artistic outcomes impact your life? Do you enjoy watching movies and the drama that often unfolds? Do you read books for pleasure? Do you have a favorite song (or songs) that are secured in the playbook of your life? Do you dance to express joy, for exercise or perhaps watch others in amazement? How often do you browse YouTube, iTunes or Vimeo for videos, music, or podcasts? Do you visit art galleries or historic properties?

The scope of methods and means of pleasures in our lives are immense. It does not matter what art form we engage in. It *does* matter if we recognize that, without the contribution of artists, the content we enjoy would be absent in our lives. Think about this.

Take a moment to write down what art forms are present in *YOUR* daily life. Query your friends for what art-centric activities they enjoy. Consider these findings as one component of evidence when developing pitches or conversing with partners and political decision makers. Build your advocacy pitch upon actual, every day, unique experiences. These can be powerful. You will want to be prepared with specific examples to use in different conversations or presentations.

When you provide an example to which your audience relates, you have their attention! Recognize this and use it as a position from which to broaden their understanding, knowledge, or partnership opportunity. Consider yourself a *transducer of knowledge*, a person who educates the general public to better understand the role of artists and the impact of art in everyone's life.

Academic literature is producing longitudinal research studies (findings developed over a long period of time) that recognize the impact of arts disciplines in patient care within the healthcare system. For example, positive cognitive activation is documented when artistic disciplines (such as music, painting, dancing) are applied in healthcare environments. The positive results are both immediate and long-term. Consider an Alzheimer's patient, "Henry," who cannot speak, for years. After listening to music channelled through headphones, he speaks in sentences and sings![xli] Or consider a Parkinson's patient in a Stanford University health study who finds it hard to walk. With the introduction of music therapy, he can somehow dance![xlii]

The study of *art for health benefits* is an area where important research is emerging. The impact of this research and resulting outcomes from case studies speak for themselves.

Comparatively, it is hard to pinpoint the return on investment in a tangible quantifiable form in these and many other social impact case studies.

In summary, artistic disciplines are being recognized and valued as important contributors to heathy minds, bodies, and communities. It is important to recognize their increasing presence along with the emerging research about this form of societal impact.

Chapter Summary

- At some level, daily, each of us sees social value and are engaged in the presence of art, either directly or indirectly.

- Social benefits related to artists' presence in our society go far beyond ticketed events, sponsorship benefits, or entertainment value. The arts are a gateway to team building, creative thinking, problem-solving, and friendship.

- The social impacts of the arts include pride in community assets; stewardship through community members; social benefits related to play, inclusion, and expression; and new relationships and partnerships between divergent stakeholders.

- Arts administrators, consider yourself a *transducer of knowledge*, a person who educates the general public in understanding the role of artists and the impact of art in everyone's life.

- In times of hardship the value of the arts and artists is appreciated. The human, emotional response to art was especially evident when COVID-19 had a stranglehold on the globe. Notably, so too was the generosity of artistic creators and arts presenters willing to console, entertain, and give hope—without consideration to monetary gain, but rather, human well-being.

- The arts connect us, whether digitally or in-person. They both complement and are a platform for how we express and experience our human connectedness.

10

In Conclusion: The (Unthinkable) Alternative

This book provides many examples of how to recognize the impact of an artist's presence in your community and everyday life — from recognizing unique assets to engaging in programming, public art, festivals, theatre, galleries, literature, community-engaged art projects, movies, contemporary art, dance, music, or singing...and the list goes on. What we do with these opportunities is an individual choice.

Another way to think about the impact of artists in your community is to consider the *absence* of artists in your community! Huh? What does this look like? Consider this:

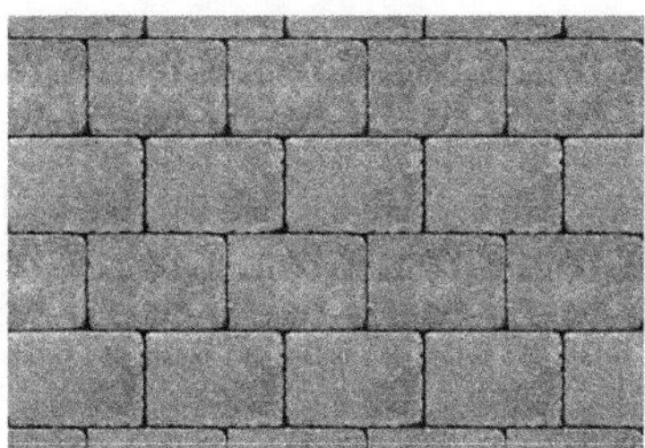

Exactly!

A world without art would be colourless. It would have no vibrancy. It would be dull. It would be void of (artistic) creative thinkers. No theatres, no movies, no books. No music, no dancing, no festivals, no galleries, no public art. No architectural character in public spaces and perhaps fewer patient advancements in health care treatments. Gala events without music, orchestras, or art auctions. Tourism sector economics would certainly be limited without the assets listed above; in fact, would tourism even exist?

We have only to think about our shared human experience of social distancing and physical isolation from each other during 2020. Think what this same experience might have looked like without access to millions of posts sharing arts-centric content we engaged with, digitally. Thinking from that perspective, we all had a glimpse of what reduced access to art forms, in the physical sense, would be like.

It is hard to visualize what our world might actually look like without access to *any* form of artistic contributions. It *is* safe to say our societies and our world would be a completely different place.

How do we further impress this stark reality upon people who do not believe in the contribution of the arts (non-arts believers)? How do we gain leverage to present the value of artists to both societies and individual lives?

A solutions-based strategy that benefits numerous stakeholders builds buy-in. Invite those who are directly impacted to suggest solutions and be involved in the decision-making process. When you establish buy-in, these constituents become your champions. Is this more work than a top-down management approach? Absolutely. However, with everyone working toward the same goal, the workload is distributed among a broader base and the probability of success increases through aggregation or a form of scalability. This solution-based strategy is aimed to work at both micro and macro levels of decision making where arts ecosystem development occurs.

Revisit the *Open House* case study to fully understand how this project reversed a negative situation into a positive outcome for multiple parties. The video is five minutes 44 seconds. A link is provided in the *References* section of this book under Chapter 7 and on the *News & Resources* at my website.

Consider a similar holistic approach in your planning, partnership development, and outcomes. Plug in the details of your community, your organization, and potential partners to develop and position yourself as 'the solution builder,' the connector, and (over time) the person or organization that partners are clamouring to team up with.

Good luck!

Afterword

The primary audience for this book is arts administrators and artists. The secondary audience is those who value local prosperity and are community builders. This latter category intuitively includes all stakeholders in a local arts ecosystem: heritage organizations and museums, residents, municipal leaders, business owners/managers, and associated provincial/state and federal government departments.

I anticipate my insights and perspectives will have varying degrees of impact depending on your perspective and the lens through which you view the arts ecosystem. I hope this book is a useful tool for arts administrators and those who want to consider working with arts administrators. I also hope it challenges established development models with an eye to cultivating new methods of holistic support, such as corporate social responsibility that includes *stakeholder capitalism* strategies and new social investment business models.

Reconsidering what drives value within the arts ecosystem and redefining (available) resources to protect and support those foundational components will make great strides to ensure the role and purpose of the artist remains intact. Opening the door to welcome non-arts-centric stakeholders who seek to generously support artists and their creative works will, undeniably, bring mutually-beneficial relationships. These supporters, with their good intentions, are waiting patiently. It is upon arts sector leaders to invite them into their milieu with curiosity and a willingness to work together. Genuine, trusting relationships will ripple in multiple directions, expanding current views of assets that broaden our visions and reshape our communities' local prosperity.

The lasting impacts of the global pandemic of COVID-19 are, at the time of this publication, unknown. What can be assured is our economies and sectors will not look the same. Businesses, arts organizations, and whole industries will endure significant losses, to varying degrees, over short-, mid-, and long-term periods. I believe this period of loss is also a period of creative deconstruction and renewal—opening our minds and resetting our values, giving rise to new ways of working together. I believe this point in history will effectively illustrate the impact and benefit of partnerships!

Thank you for investing your time, money, trust, and curiosity into this work. I am privileged to share my knowledge and insights to benefit the work of others.

I welcome your thoughts on this book through my *Get In Touch* page on my website or through email. What did you glean from this publication that you can or hope to apply to your own career? Are there particular insights that support arts sector development in your community? And please, share with me your success stories in building successful partnerships with artists and arts organizations. I would love to hear those, too.

Your stories may make it into a future book!

This book is available as an eBook in addition to the print version. Future publications, workshop information, requests for speaking engagements, or support linked to this work can be obtained through my website.

M. Catherine (Cate) Proctor, MBA
Ottawa, Ontario
Canada

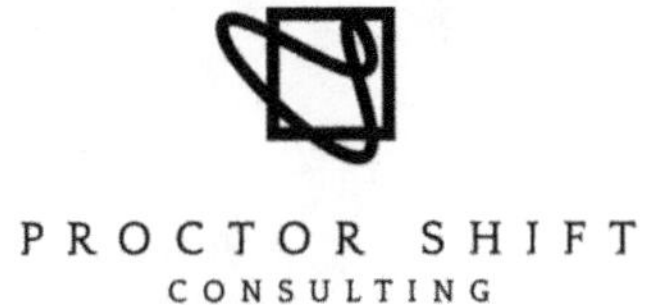

www.proctorshiftconsulting.com
cate@proctorshiftconsulting.com

References (by Chapter)

Introduction

Fisher, K., Geenen, J., Jurcevic, M., McClintock, K., & Davis, G. (2009). Applying asset-based community development as a strategy for CSR: A Canadian perspective on a win-win for stakeholders and SMEs. Oxford, UK: *Business Ethics, 18*(1), 66–72.

Lampel, J., Lant, T., & Shamsie, J. (2000). Balancing act: Learning from organizing practices in cultural industries. *Organization Science, 11*(3), 263–269.

Chapter 1

Ottawa Cultural Alliance (2019). *A liveable city for all—A new cultural roadmap for Ottawa 2019–2022.* Ottawa, ON: Ottawa Cultural Alliance. Retrieved from https://ottawaculture.ca/cultural-roadmap

Ponzini, D., & Rossi, U. (2010). Becoming a creative city: The entrepreneurial mayor, network politics and the promise of an urban renaissance. *Urban Studies, 47*(5), 1037–1057. doi: 10.1177/0042098009353073

Dabrusin, J. [Chair] (2019). *Shifting paradigms: Report of the standing committee on Canadian heritage.* Ottawa, ON: House of Commons Canada, 42nd Parliament 1st Session. Retrieved from https://www.ourcommons.ca/Content/Committee/421/CHPC/Reports/RP10481650/chpcrp19/chpcrp19-e.pdf

Chapter 2

Kronstal, K., & Grant, J. (2011). *Municipal best practices for attracting and retaining immigrant artists and cultural workers*. School of Planning, Dalhousie University *(Working Paper No.38)*. Halifax, NS: Retrieved from http://community.smu.ca/atlantic/documents/KronstalGra ntbestpractices_001.pdf

Proctor, C. (2013). *A strategic plan on arts and culture for the City of Charlottetown: A study bridging the arts and cultural community to economic development opportunities as related to the presence and utilization of creative human capital. (Unpublished master's signature project). University of Prince Edward Island, Charlottetown.* Retrieved from http://www.islandscholar.ca/islandora/search/Proctor?typ e=dismax

Fisher, K., Geenen, J., Jurcevic, M., McClintock, K., & Davis, G. (2009). Applying asset-based community development as a strategy for CSR: A Canadian perspective on a win-win for stakeholders and SMEs. Oxford, UK: *Business Ethics, 18*(1), 66–72.

V2_Lab for the Unstable Media. (1987). *Manifesto for the unstable media*. Netherlands: V2_Lab for the Unstable Media. Retrieved from https://v2.nl/archive/articles/manifesto-for-the-unstable-media

Hill Strategies. (2019a). *Estimates of the direct economic impact of culture in Canada in 2017*. Retrieved from https://hillstrategies.com/2019/06/19/estimates-of-the-direct-economic-impact-of-culture-in-canada-in-2017/

Americans for the Arts. (2019). *Arts + Social Impact Explorer*. Retrieved from https://www.americansforthearts.org/socialimpact

Hill Strategies. (2019b). *Arts + Social Impact Explorer.* Retrieved from https://hillstrategies.com/2019/10/09/arts-social-impact-explorer/

Chapter 4

Nordicity. (2019). *Making it work report--Pathways towards sustainable cultural careers. (A profile of the Cultural Sector Labour Market in Ontario, Canada.)* Toronto, ON: Work in Culture. Retrieved from https://www.workinculture.ca/getattachment/FYI/WorkInCulture-Connects/May-2019/WorkInCulture-Releases-Culture-Sector-Career-Susta/MakingItWork_Pathways-(May)-(1).pdf.aspx?lang=en-CA

The Strategic Council. (2015). *Building the case for business support of the arts.* Toronto, ON: Business for the Arts.

Lynch, R. (2013). The arts are definitely good for business
       (Special three-part series by President and CEO of
       Americans for the Arts). *Public Management, 16*(April),
       17–18. Retrieved from
       https://icma.org/sites/default/files/58_APRIL%202013%20
       %C2%B7%20VOLUME%2095%20%C2%B7%20NUMBER%20
       3.pdf

Lampel, J., Lant, T., & Shamsie, J. (2000). Balancing act: Learning
       from organizing practices in cultural industries.
       Organization Science, 11(3), 263–269.

Chapter 5

Proctor Shift Consulting (2020).
http://www.proctorshiftconsulting.com

Proctor, C. (2013). *A Strategic Plan on Arts and Culture for the
       City of Charlottetown: A study bridging the arts and cultural
       community to economic development opportunities as
       related to the presence and utilization of creative human
       capital.* (Unpublished master's signature project).
       University of Prince Edward Island, Charlottetown.
       Retrieved from
       http://www.islandscholar.ca/islandora/search/Proctor?typ
       e=dismax

The Strategic Council. (2015). *Building the case for business
       support of the arts.* Toronto, ON: Business for the Arts.

Chapter 6

Baeker, G. (2010). *Rediscovering the wealth of places—A municipal planning handbook for Canadian communities.* Union, ON: Municipal World Inc.

Chapter 7

Americans for the Arts. (2019). *Arts + Social Impact Explorer.* Retrieved from https://www.americansforthearts.org/socialimpact

Solomon, E. (2004). *The nature of economics: An interview with Jane Jacobs.* Radio interview. Toronto, ON: Canadian Broadcasting Corporation. Retrieved from https://www.cbc.ca/archives/entry/jane-jacobs-on-the-nature-of-economies

Conference Board of Canada. (2008). *Valuing culture: Measuring and understanding Canada's creative economy.* Ottawa, ON: Conference Board of Canada. Retrieved from http://www.conferenceboard.ca/e-library/abstract.aspx?did=2671

Kronstal, K., & Grant, J. (2011). *Municipal best practices for attracting and retaining immigrant artists and cultural workers (Working Paper No.38).* Halifax, NS: Dalhousie University School of Planning. Retrieved from http://community.smu.ca/atlantic/documents/KronstalGrantbestpractices_001.pdf

Markusen, A., & Schrock, G. (2006a). The distinctive city: Divergent patterns in growth, hierarchy and specialisation. *Urban Studies, 43*(8), 1301–1323. doi: 10.1080/00420980600776392

Markusen, A., & Schrock, G. (2006b). The artistic dividend: Urban artistic specialisation and economic development implications. *Urban Studies, 43*(10), 1661–1686. doi: 10.1080/00420980600888478

Mercer, C., (2013). Cultural planning and the creative economy. Weimar, DE: *Arts Management Newsletter*, 115, 4–6.

Petri, I. (2013). *The value of presenting—A study of performing arts presentation in Canada.* Ottawa, ON: Canadian Arts Presenting Association (CAPACOA). Retrieved from https://capacoa.ca/en/services/valueofpresenting/final-report

Swartz, J. (2009, Updated April 2018). *What Jane Jacobs can teach us about economics.* Santa Barbara, CA: Pacific Standard. Retrieved from http://www.psmag.com/business-economics/what-jane-jacobs-can-teach-us-about-the-economy-3383

Fisher, K., Geenen, J., Jurcevic, M., McClintock, K., & Davis, G. (2009). Applying asset-based community development as a strategy for CSR: A Canadian perspective on a win-win for stakeholders and SMEs. Oxford, UK: *Business Ethics, 18*(1), 66–72.

Hill Strategies. (2019b). Website portal to *Statistical insights on the arts. In-depth exploration of Canadian arts data.* Retrieved from https://hillstrategies.com/statistical-insights-on-the-arts/

Ottawa Cultural Alliance. (2019). *A liveable city for all—A new cultural roadmap for Ottawa 2019–2022.* Retrieved from https://ottawaculture.ca/cultural-roadmap/#after_section_1

Unison Benevolent Fund. (2020). *Mission.* Toronto, ON: Unison Benevolent Fund. Retrieved from https://unisonfund.ca/about/mission

Michel, D. (2018). *A peek behind the curtain: The expiration date on music.* Retrieved from https://www.facebook.com/therealdannymichel/posts/10160771838605467?__tn__=K-R

Mazzotta, M. (2013). *Open House.* Video. York, AL: Coleman Centre for the Arts. Retrieved from https://vimeo.com/70386286

Chapter 8

Baeker, G. (2010). *Rediscovering the wealth of places—A municipal planning handbook for Canadian communities.* Union, ON: Municipal World Inc.

Chapter 9

Crossick, G., & Kaszynska, P. (2016). *Understanding the value of arts and culture: The AHRC cultural value project*. Swindon, UK: Arts and Humanities Research Council. Retrieved from https://ahrc.ukri.org/documents/publications/cultural-value-project-final-report/

Lynch, R. (2013). The arts are definitely good for business (Special three-part series by President and CEO of Americans for the Arts). *Public Management, 16*(April), 17–18. Retrieved from https://icma.org/sites/default/files/58_APRIL%202013%20%C2%B7%20VOLUME%2095%20%C2%B7%20NUMBER%20 3.pdf

Mazzotta, M. (2013, August 12). *Open House* [Video file]. Retrieved from https://vimeo.com/70386286

Music & Memory (2010, April 13). *Alive Inside Film of Music and Memory Project – Henry's Story* [Video file]. Retrieved from https://www.youtube.com/watch?v=5FWn4JB2YLU

Richter, R. (2017). *A new rhythm: Dance benefits Parkinson's patients.* Stanford, CA: Stanford University, Stanford Medicine. Retrieved from: https://stanmed.stanford.edu/2017winter/dance-for-parkinsons-disease-at-the-stanford-neuroscience-health-center.html

Stanford Medicine (2017, February 21). *Why people with Parkinson's are dancing at Stanford's Neuroscience Health Center* [Video file]. Retrieved from https://www.youtube.com/watch?v=3BzOPrOs1E0

General References

Cray, D., & Inglis, L. (2011). Strategic decision making in arts organizations. *Journal of Arts Management, Law & Society, 41*(2), 84–102. doi: 10.1080/10632921.2011.573444

Crossan, M., Rouse, M., Fry, J., & Killing, J.P. (2013*). Strategic analysis and action.* (8th ed.) EMBA program text, University of Prince Edward Island: Pearson Canada.

Mangia, G., Canonico, P., Toraldo, M. L., & Mercurio, R. (2011). Assessing the socio-economic impact of performing arts festivals: A new theoretical model. Journal of US-China Public Administration, 8(9), 1016–1031.

Markusen, A., Wassail, G. H., DeNatale, D., & Cohen, R. (2008). Defining the creative economy: Industry and occupational approaches. *Economic Development Quarterly, 22*(1), 24–45.

Polèse, M. (2012). The arts and local economic development: Can a strong arts presence uplift local economies? A study of 135 Canadian cities. *Urban Studies, 49*(8), 1811–1835. doi: 10.1177/0042098011422574

Wenner, J. (2010). *An artistic recovery: Using arts and culture to spur economic development.* Washington, DC: Research Division, National Association of Counties, County Services Department. Retrieved from https://www.naco.org/sites/default/files/documents/An_Artistic_Recovery.pdf

Text Box (Quoted Sources):

Business/Arts, Nanos Research, & LaPlaca Cohen. (2018).
Culture track: Canada. Toronto, ON: Business for the Arts.
Retrieved from
http://www.businessandarts.org/wp-
content/uploads/2018/07/CT-Canada-Report.pdf
Raw Data to the Report is also available (open source) at
http://www.businessandarts.org/culture-track-canada/

Crossick, G., & Kaszynska, P. (2016). *Understanding the value of
arts and culture: The AHRC cultural value project.* Swindon,
UK: Arts and Humanities Research Council. Retrieved from
https://ahrc.ukri.org/documents/publications/cultural-
value-project-final-report/

Nordicity. (2019). *Making it work report: Pathways towards
sustainable cultural careers. A profile of the cultural sector
labour market in Ontario, Canada.* Toronto, ON: Work in
Culture. Retrieved from
https://www.workinculture.ca/getattachment/FYI/WorkInC
ulture-Connects/May-2019/WorkInCulture-Releases-
Culture-Sector-Career-Susta/MakingItWork_Pathways-
(May)-(1).pdf.aspx?lang=en-CA

The Strategic Council (2015). *Building the case for business
support of the arts.* Toronto, ON: Business for the Arts.

Lampel, J., Lant, T., & Shamsie, J. (2000). Balancing act: Learning
from organizing practices in cultural industries.
Organization Science, 11(3), 263–269.

Case Studies

River Arts District: Asheville, North Carolina (USA)
*RE: ARTISTS + BUSINESS + TOURISM PARTNERSHIP = AN ARTS
ECOSYSTEM*
Additional information on the River Arts District is available at
https://www.riverartsdistrict.com/

Kim's Convenience
*RE: AN ARTISTIC IDEA – REJECTED – TO AN INTERNATIONAL
TELEVISION DRAMA AWARD*
Additional information on Kim's Convenience is available at
https://www.thecanadianencyclopedia.ca/en/article/kims-
convenience

Anne of Green Gables by Lucy Maud Montgomery
*RE: FROM AN AUTHOR'S NOVEL – REJECTED - TO DRIVING A
TOURISM INDUSTRY*
Additional information on *Anne of Green Gables* and its author
is available at https://www.lmmontgomery.ca/about/lmm/her-
life
https://confederationcentre.com/whats-on/anne-of-green-
gables/
https://www.tourismpei.com/anne-of-green-gables

Open House (2013) – York, Alabama (USA)
*RE: INVITING INPUT AND INCLUSION = COMMUNITY PRIDE AND
OWNERSHIP*
Additional information on *Open House* is available at
https://vimeo.com/70386286

Art in the Open, presented by this town is small Inc. and other community members
RE: FEAR OF THE UNKNOWN versus POSITIVE EXPERIENCE BREEDS ENGAGEMENT
Additional information on the Art in the Open festival is available at https://thistownissmall.com/art-in-the-open-art-a-ciel-ouvert/

Quidi Vidi, Newfoundland, Canada
RE: CROSS-SECTORAL PARNTERSHIPS – ARTS EDUCATION, ENTREPRENEURS, MUNICIPALITY, TOURISM
Additional information on the Quidi Vidi Plantation is available at https://qvvplantation.com/

Ottawa Little Theatre – Garden Project, Ontario, Canada
RE: LEVERAGING ASSETS and COMMUNITY PARTNERSHIPS for STRATEGIC WIN, WIN, WIN!
Additional information on this urban community garden project is available at http://www.ottawalittletheatre.com/urban-community-garden-olt/

End Notes

---

[i] Fisher et al. (2009).

[ii] Based on Statistics Canada reporting, 2011

[iv] *A Liveable City for All – A New Cultural Roadmap for Ottawa 2019-2022 (2019).* Ottawa Cultural Alliance for the City of Ottawa

[v] *Becoming a Creative City – The Entrepreneurial Mayor (2010).* Ponzini & Rossi

[vi] *Shifting Paradigms (2019).* A Report of the Standing Committee on Canadian Heritage.

[vii] *Municipal Best Practices for Attracting and Retaining Immigrant Artists and Cultural Workers (2011).* Kronstal and Grant

[viii] *Trend noted while conducting my MBA research and in subsequent conversations within the sector (artists) and arts administrators.*

[ix] *A Strategic Plan on Arts and Culture for the City of Charlottetown (2013).* Proctor, C. University of Prince Edward Island Robertson Library

[x] *Manifesto For The Unstable Media (1987).* V2_Organization, Hertogenbosch (Netherlands)

https://v2.nl/archive/articles/manifesto-for-the-unstable-media

[xi] The number one barrier why Canadians do not attend arts and cultural activities. Culture Track: Canada (2018)

[xii] *Applying asset-based community development as a strategy for CSR: a Canadian perspective on a win-win for stakeholders and SME's (2009).* Fisher, K.et al. Business Ethics: A European Review

[xiii] *Estimates of the Direct Economic Impact of Culture in Canada in 2017 (2019).* Hill Strategies

xiv https://www.americansforthearts.org/socialimpact

xv *Arts + Social Impact Explorer (2019). Americans For The Arts*

xvi https://www.soulpepper.ca/about-us/our-story

xvii *Making It Work – Pathways Toward Sustainable Cultural Careers (2019).* Work in Culture

xviii Opportunity Cost: the loss of potential gain from other alternatives when one alternative is chosen, Oxford Dictionary

xix *Building The Case for Business Support of the Arts (2015).* Gregg, K., Sullivan & Woolstencroft [The Strategic Council] *Business for the Arts*

xx *The Arts Are Definitely Good For Business (2013).* Lynch, R. Public Management

xxi *Balancing Act: Learning from organizing practices in cultural industries (2000)* Lampel et al

xxii See Example within 'Artistic Driver #6 – The Artist'
xxiii *A Strategic Plan on Arts and Culture for the City of Charlottetown (2013).* Proctor, C. University of Prince Edward Island Robertson Library

xxiv *Rediscovering the Wealth of Places - A municipal cultural planning handbook for Canadian communities (2010).* Baeker, G.

xxv Compilation of References from MBA Signature Project reflecting 'The Focus Matrix' document:
Petri, I. (2013).

Kronstal, K. et al. (2011).

Markusen & Schrock (2006a).

Markusen & Schrock (2006b).

Conference Board of Canada (2008). *Valuing culture: measuring and understanding Canada's creative economy.* • ISBN 978-0-88763-832-9. Retrieved from https://www.conferenceboard.ca/temp/2bead9ec-084e-45f2-8f5a-27ffdb07177b/ 08_152%20Canada's%20Creative%20Economy_RPT_WEB.pdf

Mercer, C. (2013). *Cultural Planning and the Creative Economy (2013).* Arts Management Newsletter, Issue 115, Page 4. Retrieved from https://www.artsmanagement.net/dlf/837927fb198285467b4ca762b d41f9b3,1.pdf

June Jacobs (2004). Interview with Evan Soloman, Canadian Broadcasting Corporation
Local expert interviews (2013). Prince Edward Island: Hennessey, C., Lemm, R. (Dr.), Purdy, H.

[xxvi] Firms may find an investment in strategic analysis and social capital can pay off from a social and organizational standpoint. This combined investment will reward them with a framework for CSR providing for mutual obligation, understanding and expectations, resulting in a win-win strategy for all parties. Fisher et al. (2009).

[xxvii] Hill Strategies (2019c). Retrieved from https://hillstrategies.com/statistical-insights-on-the-arts/

[xxviii] Arts + Social Impact Explorer (2018): A tool to help people begin the journey of discovery to deeper understanding of the arts' long-term social impact.
https://www.americansforthearts.org/socialimpact,

[xxix] Crossick et al. (2016).

[xxx] An example of 'next generation' planning is outlined in the creation of The New Ottawa Cultural Roadmap, facilitated and presented by the Ottawa Cultural Alliance. https://ottawaculture.ca/cultural-roadmap/#after_section_1

[xxxi] Canadian Association for the Performing Arts. www.capacoa.ca

[xxxii] <u>Relationship marketing</u> is a strategy designed to foster customer loyalty, interaction and long-term engagement. It is designed to develop strong connections with customers by providing them with information directly suited to their needs and interests and by promoting open communication. https://www.forbes.com/sites/marketshare/2013/05/09/this-is-the-most-important-word-when-it-comes-to-relationship-marketing/#73d857069e61

[xxxiii] Whittaker, M. (2020). Is COVID-19 Killing Shareholder Primacy? https://www.forbes.com/sites/martinwhittaker/2020/04/09/is-covid-19-killing-shareholder-primacy/#36c8d2ef5661

[xxxiv] Danny Michel (2018). https://www.facebook.com/therealdannymichel/posts/10160771838605467?__tn__=K-R

[xxxv]Unison Benevolent Fund (2020). https://unisonfund.ca/about/mission

[xxxvi] Open House (2011). An artist-in-residence program that combined residents' input with municipal, engineering, and community effort. The project redeveloped a dilapidated property into a community public park for concerts, movies and public events.

[xxxvii] Baeker (2010).

[xxxviii] Crossick et al. (2016).

[xxxix] Public Management (2012).

[xl] Mazzotta, M (2013). *Open House*

[xli] Music & Memory (2010). *Alive Inside Film of Music and Memory Project – Henry's Story*

[xlii] Stanford Medicine (2017). *Why people with Parkinson's are dancing at Stanford's Neuroscience Health Center*